T0003882

THE LITTLE BLACK BOOK OF
FLY FISHING

THE LITTLE BLACK BOOK OF
FLY FISHING

201 TIPS TO MAKE YOU A BETTER ANGLER

Kirk Deeter
and
Chris Hunt

Skyhorse Publishing

Skyhorse Publishing books may be purchased in bulk at special discounts for sales promotion, corporate gifts, fund-raising, or educational purposes. Special editions can also be created to specifications. For details, contact the Special Sales Department, Skyhorse Publishing, 307 West 36th Street, 11th Floor, New York, NY 10018 or info@skyhorsepublishing.com.

Skyhorse® and Skyhorse Publishing® are registered trademarks of Skyhorse Publishing, Inc.®, a Delaware corporation.

Visit our website at www.skyhorsepublishing.com.

10 9 8 7 6 5 4 3 2 1

Library of Congress Cataloging-in-Publication Data is available on file.

Cover design by Mona Lin
Cover art credit: Getty Images

Print ISBN: 978-1-5107-4773-9
Ebook ISBN: 978-1-5107-4774-6

Printed in China

THIS BOOK IS DEDICATED TO THE
LATE, GREAT CHARLIE MEYERS.

Contents

Foreword

I don't have a lot of fly-fishing tips, as I'm a bit of a scrounger. I've taken as many tips from Kirk Deeter and Chris Hunt's writing, TV shows like the *New Fly Fisher*, the *Orvis Guide to Fishing*, and Jose Wejebe's *Spanish Fly*, along with dozens of other sources, as I could over the last decade or so. I can unequivocally say I learned the most about fly fishing while trying to implement something taught to me by a guide. Ten years on since the debut of *The Little Red Book of Fly Fishing*, I finally have a tip I fully believe in to share. It won't result in more hookups for you necessarily, but it will get you out on the water more, and it will do something phenomenal for fly fishing. It'll grow the sport.

When I travel, I often book a full day of guided fishing. If my brother couldn't join me, I used to selfishly keep the second spot unfilled. In my zeal to learn, I craved the full attention of my guide. Now I look for a young person of color who has raised their hand and invite them to fish with me as my guest. I'm African American, and I know that as of this writing, there are fewer Blacks, Hispanics, and Asians engaging fly fishing (and there never have been that many of us to begin with). I've been blessed by learning the sport, growing a deep conservation ethic. Fly fishing has taken me around the world and helped me find new friends and mentors in life. So the tip I can offer is to give back to the sport we so cherish by taking the next step to become a mentor to a new angler.

My guidance to you is that you find the person who could use the river, flat, and bow most in your life and take them fly fishing. It'll be a disaster at first, but a wonderful, sloppy, spine-tingling one. Even if all they learn to do is stand in a flowing river and observe the pressure of the current on their legs, you'll both be better for it. Perhaps they'll see through the water and spot their first trout. Perhaps they'll take notice of the dropping tide and ask about the dark shadows on the edges of the mangrove. Maybe they'll enjoy the rhythm of the cast— "tick-tock"—or notice the sound of silence on the ride back to the dock. And perhaps they'll want to do it again.

My top three favorite tips in this book in the following order are 1) Get Out of Your Comfort Zone, 2) Urban Angling, and 3) I Cheer for the Fish. When you're taking a new angler out, you'll often find yourself back at the town lake, well, in the middle of town. Abundant with bream and sunnies, eager to hit a fly. It'll feel weird, maybe uncomfortable as you might be the only one with a fly rod. But stride in there like you own it. Tie nothing less than a blue Bogglebug on 4x with a short seven-foot six-inch 2-weight glass rod (pro tip: use an unweighted damselfly nymph as a dropper), and put that rod in your mentee's hands. When they miss the first electrifying strike, cheer for them, then cheer for the fish! Remind your mentee that if it was supposed to be easy they'd call it catching and not fishing.

You'll revel in Chris and Kirk's *The Little Black Book of Fishing*, because you're going to quickly see the secret plan of their book. You see, these tips were meant to be passed on.

Damn, I think I just gave it away.

—Joel R. Johnson

Introduction

Everything in the fly-fishing world is connected in one way or another.

The number one lesson I have learned since Charlie Meyers and I wrote The *Little Red Book of Fly Fishing* over ten years ago is that fly fishing isn't only about fish . . . or flies . . . or casts . . . or any of that. It's about the places you see, and the people you meet along the way. Charlie knew that all along. He was a wonderful mentor and, in more ways than you might imagine, he still is.

The prompt for that *Little Red Book* was a road trip Charlie and I took to Wyoming. He told me (didn't ask) that we had to visit the Wyoming Range to help Trout Unlimited and others save a sacred bastion of cutthroat trout—he'd cover for the *Denver Post*, and me for *Field & Stream* magazine. And when we rolled into basecamp after a hot, dusty ride in Charlie's gray Jeep Cherokee, we were met by one Chris Hunt, who instantly handed us each a glass of high-end bourbon on ice. That was how I was introduced to Mr. Hunt. I liked him immediately, of course, but truth be told, in hindsight, I realize now that half of the reason Charlie dragged me along on that story was the angle itself, and the other half was because he wanted to make the connection between me and Chris.

Charlie and I wrote our Wyoming Range stories. TU eventually won the day on that deal (thanks to Chris, Tom Reed, and others). And from there (literally starting on the through-the-night drive home) Charlie and I continued to noodle around on the *Little Red Book* idea—the whole point of which was to open our respective notebooks and convey some simple tips and ideas we'd picked up during our travels.

Fly fishing isn't rocket science. A lot of people have made a lot of money explaining just how complicated it is . . . and Charlie and I both fundamentally felt that was a load of bull. Nobody's a complete expert. And the more you fish, the more you realize just how much you still have to learn. That said, we felt that a few tips gleaned over some hard-earned miles from a couple humble reporters might just help shorten the learning curve for some. So, we spilled our beans, the *Red Book* was born, and that was that.

Sadly, Charlie died of lung cancer (the nonsmoker variety) before he ever saw that book in print. But the seeds got planted. His influence has never waned, not one bit.

Chris Hunt and I stayed in touch. We did more stories together. He brought me along on a *Field&Stream*/TU collaboration profiling the "Best Wild Places" in America, which I think still stands as one of the best, most far-reaching defenses of both public lands and native trout species ever documented. Eventually, Chris actually hired me into the Trout Unlimited fold. We've since fished many places together, from the wilds of Lake Athabasca in Saskatchewan to the flats off Long Island in the Bahamas. And we've continued to fight hard to protect trout and salmon waters throughout North America for the past several years.

Having said all that, I have always known that if I ever did a sequel to *The Little Red Book of Fly Fishing*, I would do it with Chris Hunt, because that's who Charlie Meyers would have wanted me to do it with.

So here we are, more than ten years after that first book. Funny thing is . . . that *Little Red Book* became somewhat of a cult classic, and it vaulted me to places—to catch fish and write stories about all that—I would never have imagined when I was a young man just starting down the angling path along the Baldwin River in northern Michigan. Places like the Fjordlands of New Zealand and the Central Highlands of Tasmania, to the jungles and pampas of South America . . . Iceland, Ireland, Siberian Russia . . . and pristine bonefish flats scattered around two oceans. I've been very lucky.

And by the same token, Chris's writing prowess has led him on similar paths throughout the world. Which is a shrinking world, in the fly-fishing sense, even given all that's going on now.

I would humbly suggest that you not assume that I (nor Chris) have actually gotten "smarter" through all these travels. Every step I take out of the comfort zone, I realize just how much I still have to learn.

That said, the well did get quite a bit deeper. The notebooks got a lot thicker. There are an awful lot of things happening on the other sides of the world that American anglers can learn from, and apply to their fishing right here, with great effect. The more I listened to people from other countries and applied that to my fishing back home (still, for the record, the answer to the "If you had one day to fish anywhere in the world?" question is my home water) . . . well, the better I got. Chris would say the same.

And so we made this the *Little Black Book,* not so much to be a collection of "dirty little secrets" or contacts. Rather, we think the tips herein are kicked up a level with a little more "worldly" view—still mostly trout-centric, but with a few added little bits from the flats, jungles, pike lakes, and carp spots. If the *Red Book* was meant to get you on the slopes in the first place, this book might put you on some more "expert" terrain. Think black diamond.

For some of you, there's going to be some stuff that still seems elementary. Some tips might be forehead-slappers and reminders. Yet sometimes we might take you to places you hadn't thought of before. If that happens a few times or more, that's all we're hoping for. After all, true expertise in fly fishing is not only the ability to push the envelope, but also the willingness to revisit and reconsider some basics as you do so. It's a cumulative deal.

And the most positive "cumulative" effect any angler can realize—aside from the fancy flick casts, or wowza bug patterns you might encounter—is to collect the sights, sounds, smells, tastes and most important, the personalities you meet along the way, and hold them all sacred.

What goes around comes around, especially in fly fishing. And it's a smaller world—even more beautiful and even more filled with opportunity, adventure, and great friends whom you will remember and respect for your entire life—than you can even imagine now. It all ties together. Get after those connections. That's the ultimate "black diamond" tip for fly fishing. Trust me.

—Kirk Deeter, Steamboat Springs, Colorado, *June 2021*

PART ONE

Casting

1. Great Casts Are the Ones That Get Bit

So much emphasis in the fly-fishing world is placed on the importance of being able to cast well. And there are many great teachers, such as John Juracek, Steve Rajeff, and others, who have really perfected not only the art of casting, but also the art of *explaining* casting.

Admittedly, I'm more of a fisherman than a caster. I believe you should definitely work on, hone, and tune your cast as much as you feel like doing so, because that's fun. And feeling the rod load just right, and tossing a perfect loop is as much an accomplishment as busting a three-hundred-yard drive right down the middle of the fairway.

But you don't need to have a perfect cast to catch fish. Not on the river with trout, nor even on the saltwater flats (but I will say the casting part is ten times more critical in saltwater than it is on a river). A great cast will never hurt you, of course, but that is NOT the price of admission to being a highly successful fly angler.

Do I say this to discourage people from working on their casts? Absolutely not. But if you're a newbie, or an intermediate, or even a self-professed expert, and you run into someone who tells you your cast isn't very good according to the "textbooks," don't be discouraged. Rather, ask yourself one simple question. Can my cast catch fish or not? If the answer is "yes," great, you're on the advanced track. There's a whole bunch of other stuff to worry about that matters much more than how pretty the loops over your head look. —**KD**

2. Everybody Needs a Casting Lesson. Everybody.

During a visit to Island Park, Idaho, not long ago, I had the chance to watch John Juracek instruct a group of anglers with varying degrees of casting ability. John is one of the few really good casting instructors who can help anyone—and I mean anyone—become a better caster in short order.

After putting all of the students through the paces and helping them identify areas where they needed to improve, John put folks like me and fellow editor/angler Kirk Deeter on the spot. He had us take the practice rod and demonstrate our own technique to the class of students. It was eye-opening.

Like a lot of anglers who have been fly fishing for decades, I realized that I had developed some long-term flaws in my cast—for me, my biggest problem is with the propensity to

acquire wind knots in my tippet after trying to perform longer casts. John was quick to point out that my elbow was too low when I was casting, and that I often tried to cast a loop that was just too tight—that resulted in the knots (note: wind knots aren't a thing—flaws in the casts that make wind knots happen *are* a thing!).

Since that "kick the tires" lesson from John, I've become much more aware of where my elbow is when I'm casting longer lines and, as a result, I'm changing my tippet less frequently thanks to wind knots.

The moral of this story? Don't turn down a casting lesson from an expert. Maybe you have twenty years of fly casting under your belt, but chances are you've developed some bad habits over those twenty years. Everybody needs a fly-casting lesson. —**CH**

THE LITTLE BLACK BOOK OF FLY FISHING

3. The Casting Practice Drills I Still Do at Least Once a Month

These are three drills I've talked about for years, but worth mentioning again because an angler can never outgrow them. 1) Take a long piece of rope, or old fly line, or a measuring tape and make a straight line on the ground. Now take your rod and flick it back and forth at waist level (parallel to the ground) so you can see the loops form a perfect U. Too much oomph, a tailing loop. Too little stop and start, an open loop. Once you have those loops uniform, take that cast up overhead where it belongs. 2) Forty feet in four seconds. Set out three targets forty feet away, and practice banging casts on those targets within four seconds, starting with the fly in your hand. 3) Strip out forty feet of line and pile it at your feet. Now, starting with fly in hand and letting go, false cast back and forth until you pick up that whole line, feeling the starts and stops, but also the slowing of the overall casting tempo as you cast longer line. Drill those regularly and the cast becomes instinct, but you still need to brush up now and then. Everyone does. —**KD**

4. Score Casts Like You Would Golf Strokes

I've often thought that golf and fly fishing are very similar. Both attract the same mindset of "problem-solver" type-A people who are into making a mark. Both sports were born in Scotland centuries ago at around the same time (though there is evidence that certain tribes in the Amazon rain forest tied bright bird feathers to hooks fashioned from shells many centuries ago). If you ask how much time in a given golf round is actually dedicated to making a swing, it would be seconds or minutes against hours. Same should be true for fly fishing.

There's a silly notion that you need to "cover water" and drop flies into every darn place where you think a trout might be hiding. I suppose that's fine. Take your chances.

But I am more into the idea of dropping a fly into a spot where opportunity legitimately knocks. So I wonder if more fly casters shouldn't hold off and drop a shot where they think it really belongs, rather than putting a cast where they might think something could happen.

Nothing wrong with the latter, mind you, but I'm into higher odds. Anglers who routinely fire casts into blank spaces might actually be better off if they hold back and make one good cast really count, as opposed to making three warmup casts.

Think of it like golf. It's the same sport, one played wet, the other played dry (though in my case, with golf, they're often equally wet). But imagine if anglers scored their casts like golf strokes. Nature, and the trout, are doing that already. The fewer the better. As soon as you start thinking about fly casts, false casts or otherwise, like golf strokes, the lower (and better) your overall score will be. —**KD**

5. **A Double Haul Is Really Important, and Not Just in the Salt**

After years and years of chasing trout and freshwater fish, I finally got the opportunity to travel to the Bahamas some years back. And on my first saltwater trip, I didn't catch a single bonefish. I did manage to catch ladyfish, small tarpon, and snappers, but these fish were caught in canals with noticeable and detectable currents—you know, kind of like trout water.

Yes, the weather on this trip was miserable. But there were bonefish to be caught. And, because I was just learning the ins and outs of double hauling, I was at a distinct disadvantage, both in the wind, and because I simply couldn't reach fish that were just a bit off their feeding routine due to the unsettled weather.

A few months after that first saltwater trip, I ran into the esteemed fly-casting instructor Ed Jaworowski and mentioned to him that I really needed to hone my double haul. We were in New Orleans, and I was about to embark on a marsh trip to chase redfish. If ever I needed the improved distance on my cast, this was the moment.

Ed and I stood at the casting pond at the fly-fishing convention we were both attending, and within five minutes, I was double hauling and had added several feet to my cast.

Today, I use the double-haul cast whenever I'm lucky enough to go and chase saltwater fish, but it's also become a more intuitive cast that I find myself unconsciously incorporating into just about every aspect of my fishing, from chasing pike on Reindeer Lake in Saskatchewan to casting to trout from the bow of a driftboat or chasing rangy carp in the shallows of the Snake River. The added ability to battle the wind and to lengthen my cast has undoubtedly resulted in more hookups.

That's the funny thing about casting. The more you do it, the more you add to your casting toolbox. If you don't know how to double haul, learn it. It's not just for saltwater fly fishing. —**CH**

6. Troubleshooting the Haul: Don't Let Those Hands Fly Far Apart

Chris is right. Hauling helps any cast because it loads the rod more effectively, and if you can feel that in your hands, you'll generate more line speed and make more accurate and powerful casts. The one problem a lot of casters make, however, is to let their arms fly apart too far when they're hauling. I'll take a subtle "mini-haul" where my hands get no farther than a foot apart, and all I'm doing with the non-casting hand

is tugging on the line, not making a big, exaggerated, wide, and wild haul that that's hard to harness and often lets the energy out of the load. —**KD**

7. **Your Casting Stroke Should Follow Your Joints, in Order, by Size**

Let me try to unravel that by saying that I was fine-tuning my cast with the help of John Juracek, who teaches out of West Yellowstone. John noticed that I was letting my elbow get ahead of my shoulder sometimes, meaning I was using my elbow to power the cast, and that was costing me distance. He said that if you let your shoulder provide the foundational power for the casting stroke, then add the elbow, and then add just a little bit of wrist at the end, then you will form tighter, more wind-efficient and distance-covering loops. Shoulder, elbow, wrist, in that order. If you look at people having trouble with the cast, I'll bet you nine out of ten are over-elbowing, over-wristing, or not following the rhythm of their joints according to size. My family has an old farm bell that I ring by pulling on a rope. If I stand with my back to the bell, and pull that rope with my casting arm, I naturally start with the shoulder, add a little elbow, and finish with some wrist. Imagine yourself ringing that bell when you cast, and your line will travel farther and straighter. —**KD**

8. **Bad Cast? Fish It Anyway**

My nineteen-year-old daughter had driven over from her summer gig in the Tetons to chase some native cutthroats with me at our favorite little haunt high in the Caribou Range of eastern Idaho, and the fish were cooperating.

Delaney was using her tenkara rod—she can cast a traditional fly rod, but the tenkara rod is her favorite. It's simple, packable, and generally foolproof, especially on small water where fly line has a knack for finding overhanging willows and getting caught on rocks and snags at your feet.

She and I had spotted a sizable cutty holding and sipping crippled caddis under the shade of streamside willows about thirty feet upstream, and if she was going to make the cast to that fish, she'd have to move her feet first. She's a pretty intuitive angler, but she still asks questions, which is a good thing. But the tenkara rod limited her distance, and she showed surprising grace navigating the creek's slippery rocks on her way to a reasonable casting position in a pair of old sandals.

Oh, to be young again.

Set up slightly downstream and across from the working cutthroat—and still unnoticed by the fish, judging from its regular rises beneath the willows—she knew she'd have to make a solid cast to get a look. With her thirteen-foot-long tenkara rod, she started false casting a Size 14 brown caddis, a reasonable imitation of the bugs that were climbing out of the creek and occupying the streamside vegetation. They were everywhere, and the cutthroats were into them.

Her first cast was spot-on, and the drift, using the long, supple rod, was ideal. But it didn't get a look. After the fly drifted through the sweet spot, she lightly lifted the line off the water and recast. This effort was short of the target by about two feet, but I figured it would at least get a solid drift.

She went to pick up the line, but I interjected.

"Leave it," I said. "Just let it drift. You don't want to spook the fish."

Especially when fishing dry flies, it can be crucial to let an errant cast drift through your target water even when it's a little (or a lot) off the mark. Frustration can often tempt us to rip a cast that lands far shy of its target off the water for a prompt recast, but doing so can easily and often put down not just the individual fish you may have been targeting—but any others that may be lurking beneath the surface as well. When that happens, it won't matter how good your next cast is.

She lowered the rod tip and let the caddis drift. We both watched as the big cutthroat left the shadows of the over-hanging brush and charged after the dry fly. She connected and moments later, she showed off her catch.

The lesson? Sometimes fly fishing can be just like horse-shoes or hand grenades. It doesn't always have to be perfect, it just has to be close. Fishing a bad cast through the drift can sometimes result in surprising results. Often, I've had short casts or long casts result in solid hookups, and sometimes with fish I wasn't even targeting. —CH

9. Five Feet Short on Purpose

We've all been told not to false cast directly over a fish we're targeting (that's upstream and facing away) because that could spook them. Makes perfect sense, right? I've always thought it

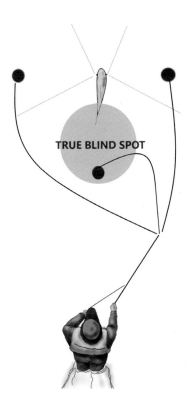

TRUE BLIND SPOT

best to false cast off to the side a bit, and then drop the fly on the fish when ready. But I've soured on that a bit and here's why: Most fish have eyes on the sides of their heads, so they can see to either side. But they can't see through their tails. Their true blind spot is directly behind them. So it makes sense to false cast right behind the fish, just about five feet short. Err on the side of caution, so start ten feet short, and gradually let out line with the line-managing finger on your rod grip (or your hauling hand if you manage line distance that way). All you really need to do is shoot about five feet of line on the final cast—that's just over half a rod length. Anyone can do that, especially with a little practice. I've learned that rather than trying to measure out the perfect distance off to the side, I'm better off false casting an imperfect, intentionally short distance right behind the fish, getting the angle right, staying in the blind spot, and then shooting out a few feet of line at the end. I spook far fewer rising fish that way. —**KD**

10. **Make Your Only Cast Count**

Kirk makes a good point above, but we're not completely on the same page here, and that's OK. For me, even five feet, particularly with big, smart trout with really good peripheral vision, is too close. Often, when fishing to graduate-level trout, you're only going to get one cast. It's important to make that one cast count.

Here's what I do.

If I spy a rising fish in a tough spot, I don't risk putting the fish down or spooking it by simply eyeballing the distance and making the cast right away. Instead, I'll throw a cast as far away from the working fish as I can, but try to make that cast perfect when it comes to distance and presentation.

Call it a warm-up swing, if you will.

For instance, I was fishing the Colon Curra in Patagonia several years back, and my guide, Peter, walked me up a froggy slough where we saw a really nice brown trout rising fairly regularly in deep water near an undercut bank and under an overhanging willow branch. If I flubbed the cast, chances are the big brown would have simply dropped to the bottom and stayed there. My chance would have been blown.

Instead, I gauged the distance between me and the fish and picked a spot about thirty feet upstream of my target. I walked up a bit and made a few casts. Adjusting for distance, I landed the last cast about three inches from the bank. Perfect.

Taking care not to reel in, but instead strip line in, I moved back downstream and repeated the last cast I made to my imaginary target. The hopper landed with an audible "splat" inches from the bank and drifted perfectly under the overhanging willow.

And, yes, the big brown ate it.

When you get only one shot, you want to make sure you're giving yourself the *best* shot. —**CH**

11. **Teaching Someone New? Start with Tenkara**

Over the last decade or so, the tenkara fly-fishing "discipline" has arrived and flourished on Western shores. Tenkara is an ancient Japanese fly-fishing method that incorporates a long, supple rod (eleven to thirteen feet or so), a line, and a leader. There is no reel.

At first blush, it might seem a little too simple. But it works, and it often works better than conventional fly casting because it's much easier for anglers to achieve full line control. It's possible, using a tenkara rod, to have only the fly on the water, which takes the drag out the equation altogether.

Where I've found this method particularly useful is when I'm fishing with new fly fishers. This technique allows new anglers to learn some of the more subtle nuances of fly fishing without having to worry about line control, a drag-free drift, or that perfect reach cast. Instead, they're focused on reading the water, identifying quality holding habitat, and perfecting a simple forward cast.

I love to fish with a tenkara rod, and over the years, I've caught significant trout using this method—it's not just for small fish. And, frankly, it's not just for trout. Kirk and I, on a trip to Lake Athabasca years ago, when tenkara was a budding "fad," managed to boat northern pike on a tenkara rod (until Kirk hooked a beast of a pike that was just too much for the lightweight instrument), and then landed an eight-pound lake trout as it migrated up a small stream to spawn.

It's fun, but it's also a great learning tool. Young anglers, in particular, tend to gravitate to tenkara simply because of all the things it lacks, like the reel, the need to control line with the off hand, and the need to worry about drag. —**CH**

12. **Be Lefty in the Salt, and Rajeff on a River**

One could argue that nobody influenced more casters—through print, video, or in person—than Lefty Kreh. I was fortunate to have been introduced to Lefty by Terry Gunn, legendary guide from Lees Ferry, Arizona, who is also one of the best casters I know (almost as good as his wife, Wendy).

Lefty could talk to an audience, and unfurl a cast, semi-sidearm, and drop a piece of yarn on a dinner plate, even when he was ninety years old.

Steve Rajeff is probably one of the three purest casters I've ever seen. He and his brother Tim can both bomb it, but Steve has a very precise, upright, "pick it up and set it down" motion, and he can do that at, say, sixty feet with such accurate aplomb that he rarely missed, and won many casting contests in the process.

I tried to learn from and emulate them both. I love these casting styles in equal measure.

But I've learned to emulate one or the other, depending on where I am and what I am fishing for. When I'm on the front of a flats skiff, I open my body, double-haul, and fire that line like Lefty (or as close as I can be). I'm a three-quarter-angle pitcher and let it rip. In the fresh, however, I aspire to emulate Rajeff; straight up and down, pointed on a clear linear angle at the target. If you can be Lefty in the salt and Rajeff in the fresh (Google them, watch them), you can cast to and hook any fish, anywhere in the world. —**KD**

13. **Casting Longer Leaders**

Several years ago, while visiting Patagonia in the Argentinian fall, my guide insisted that I cast a long leader for the brook trout we were pursuing in the Rio Corcovado. Here at home, I usually cast a nine-foot leader, with maybe eighteen inches of tippet. On the Corcovado, my leader was likely closer to eighteen feet.

And I hated it! I really struggled with the long leader, the lead fly, and the dropper—it was completely uncomfortable for me. I just couldn't slow my casting motion enough to effectively make a dependable presentation.

Over the course of an afternoon, though, I figured out how to fling that long leader with some semblance of accuracy. I took to actually watching my backcast so I knew (and couldn't just feel) when my rod was loaded. I would watch over my shoulder as the long leader unfolded behind me. Then, and only then, would I continue my forward cast.

It's one thing to tell an angler to "just slow your cast down," and another thing to actually do it. For one, such a long leader makes for a cast that just isn't intuitive to a lot of us. But there are benefits to using long leaders, not the least of which is the ability to put flies over spooky fish without "lining them" with heavy fly line.

I'm still not a long-leader fan (likely because my backcountry cutthroats here in eastern Idaho don't require so much stealth), but I have gotten better at casting long leaders. For me the solution was a visual one—I needed to be able to see the leader unfold.

Next time you're struggling with a long leader, try watching your backcast until you get a better feel for the needed casting speed. —**CH**

14. How to Cast a Fifteen-Foot Leader (and Why)

In places like New Zealand, a longer leader and tippet is considered vital. They want to keep the actual fly line as far away from the target fish as possible, and nine feet doesn't do that as well as fifteen feet. I don't know if I'm that sensitive myself, but I have been using longer leaders, especially when I'm fishing dries on

clear water, and one thing is becoming clear: The longer leader cannot hurt your odds *if you know how to cast one.*

The key to casting a longer leader is to build a longer leader that's easier to cast. So I do favor a very heavy butt section, and I'll build down to my desired diameter from there. Knotted leaders are fine if you are going long; if I want to end up with 5X, for example, I'll start that leader with 2X, and build out three-foot intervals (stepping down 2X, 3X, 4X. . .) with blood knots.

With longer leaders, you really need to mind your form and not over-wrist the cast. Easy, gentle, technical strokes are called for, because punching the line creates tailing loops, and the potential mess is increased incrementally the longer the leader.

Lastly, you want to adjust the plane of your cast so everything is fully extended about two feet above the surface—you can't be having that long leader extend six feet and drop to the surface, or it's going to recoil, and you lose the whole reason for fishing a longer leader. The exception is if you want some coils of loose tippet to absorb some current as the fly drifts. That's another useful move with the long leader, and in that case all you want to do is have the whole line and leader fully extend just a bit higher above the water surface. —**KD**

15. **Beating the Wind**

Nobody knows how to manage casts in wind better than the guides in the Bahamas. It's almost always puffing at least a little bit in the "Out" Islands. My friend Paul Zabel told me the story about how he was choking with his cast in the wind, but his guide wasn't buying the excuses. To prove the point, the guide climbed down off the poling platform, slipped the boat in gear, pointed straight into the breeze, then told Paul to hold that course with the wheel. He then proceeded to stand on the front deck and cast perfect tight loops until the backing knot popped through the rod tip.

"Rude boy, soft boy" Torrie Bevans told me once in a similar scenario on South Andros. You're aggressive on the backcast, and gentle on the forward cast. Hard . . . easy. Completely counterintuitive, because you want to punch that cast into the wind. But good casts are all about well-formed loops, stopping and starting the rod, and line speed. The wind in your face is going to help you generate line speed, especially if you start the cast and load the rod with the tip at or near the water. Then it's just a matter of grabbing the

Casting

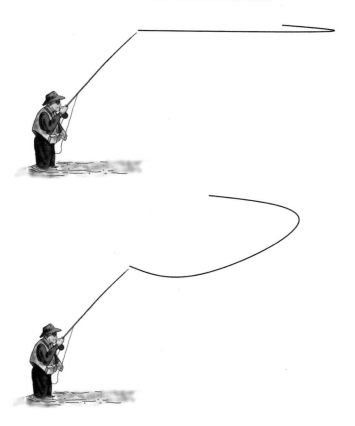

extended line behind you and redirecting it forward with a soft and purposeful motion. You don't need to add any mustard at that point. The backcast is the engine, the forward stroke is the steering wheel. And the wind is your friend; it gives you almost all the fuel you need. —**KD**

16. "Casting" Nymphs Under Indicators

A lot of anglers don't fish with indicators when they're drifting nymphs through likely runs, and that's totally fine. Others do, and today's bulky, high-floating indicators can work against a traditional fly cast. In fact, with a two-nymph rig in deep water, using an indicator, I don't think I'd even try a traditional cast.

Well-known guide Rod Patch, who knows both the Henry's Fork and the Green River like few others, showed me a method years ago of nymphing deep water under an indicator that I still use today. What's more, when I'm fishing with new anglers, I share this method with them, and I've watched as many have enjoyed some success with it.

First, ditch the idea of an upstream cast. Assuming your nymph (or nymphs) is, say, three to four feet under your indicator and you're fishing a nine-foot leader, simply let the appropriate amount of line out and let it and your leader/tippet/flies drift downstream below you. Point your rod tip downstream so your fly rod and your line come together to form a straight line. The friction of the current should be stretching the nymphs out below you.

Let's say you're standing in the stream and the current is running right to left, and let's say you're a right-handed caster. With your rod and line both pointed downstream, simply lift your right elbow and turn your right wrist out. Using the friction generated by your fly line and your nymph rig, simply lift and flip, bringing your casting arm in front of you from left to right. This will bring your line up and on its way upstream of you, where the fly (or flies) will drift through the strike zone.

If you're a left-handed caster, it's even easier. Just rotate your left wrist so your palm is up, and lift and flip. Voilà! A cast. Without actually casting. —**CH**

17. Red Book Reminder: Keep That Thumb in Your Peripheral Vision

Of all the tips in the *Little Red Book of Fly Fishing*, the one casting tip that has been most talked about, absorbed, and appreciated by readers and people in the audience when I'm giving a talk somewhere is the simple little ditty by the late Dan Stein, who guided on the Bighorn. If you keep your thumb in your peripheral vision as you cast, you solve many problems at once—like over-cocking the wrist, going back too far with the backcast, and letting your arm swing wildly away from your body. That one little tip is the one I think about most myself, and share most often, even now, so it gets a follow-up mention in this book too. It is, at once, one of the simplest and one of the most advanced teaching tips you'll ever hear about casting fly rods. I was lucky to hear that one from Dan. —**KD**

18. The Cast-Killer

I know many good fly casters, and all of them have a little hitch in their giddyup. I sure do (they just change every now and then. Usually after I sort one out, I develop another). But there's one overriding, subtle goof that separates those who think they are great casters and those who really are great casters when it comes to seizing the moment and dropping the fly on a feeding fish, right on time and on target.

That flaw is that is dropping the tip of the rod at the end of the cast. A lot of people can form a tight loop and cover sixty feet no problem. But when it's time to drop it on the money, some of the best anglers throw the tip toward the water.

It's a natural reaction! Point at the fish! But I'm telling you, you need to stop the rod at least a few feet above the waterline and have the trust that the leader and tippet will straighten out, and deliver the fly on your behalf.

Stop the rod, and don't let that rod tip flutter down toward the water surface like the fly itself. You might want the fly to seem lifeless, but you don't want to take the life out of the cast. The only things that should fall are the line, leader, tippet, and fly or flies. If those things fall in the wrong place, let the fly settle and drift out, and cast again. Don't pile drive that cast and don't drop the tip of the rod. If you do, you lose all accuracy, all purpose, and you're just left adrift. Control your destiny with a good, crisp cast that stops above the waterline. —**KD**

19. **Get a Practice Rod**

Practice rods are great little implements that anglers can use just about anywhere, and at any time. They're compact, affordable, and they are very visual—with a practice rod, you can literally see how you're casting and work, largely on your own, to iron out any issues with your overall fly cast. What's the first thing I look for when I try and troubleshoot my own cast? See Kirk's tip above that I first saw in the *Red Book* he and Charlie wrote.

There are several models of casting rods available, and they all tend to do generally the same thing—assist you in keeping your cast sharp (even when, say, it's 11°F outside and the river is covered with ice and snow) and your eye keen to see problems. I use mine probably four times a week when I need to keep my hands busy. —**CH**

20. **Don't Outkick Your Coverage**

The old adage goes that the sixty-yard punt is a great thing until the team realizes there's nobody downfield to cover immediately, and then the returner wiggles loose and sprints down the sideline for a touchdown.

The funny thing with anglers is that they use the distance of their cast as a measure of proficiency. "Wow, she can cast ninety feet, she's really good!" Well, she probably is a really good caster, but the jury might be out on what kind of an angler she is. Because expert anglers actually are more interested in seeing how short a cast they can get away with, and don't really give a rip about making those long hero casts.

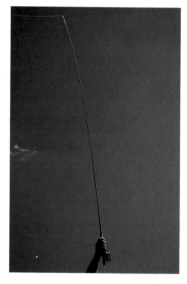

At least that's true on most trout rivers. Salt water is a different game with different rules. A long cast is often the price of admission on the flats. But on a trout river, it's often dumb to cast far.

It's hard to set a Size 18 dry-fly hook, for example, from sixty feet away (if you're going to try, a swift down-current directional jerk at waist level is better than lifting over your head). Even if you hook up, it's hard to keep tension, steer the fish, fight the fish, gather the slack, and more. You simply outkick your coverage at that distance, and there are few reasons to do it. Maybe there's a fish rising on the other side of a deep current, and you can't wade into range. Fine, take your best shot, but you're going to have about two seconds of presentation max before the current grabs the line.

Great casting is really all about positioning, and I wish more anglers would equate a fly cast more with throwing darts than hitting a driver on the golf course. —**KD**

21. **Learn to Spey Cast**

I've never been much of a steelhead guy. I live in Idaho, where we do have an iconic run of chromers that swim more than eight hundred miles from the ocean to the Salmon and Clearwater rivers to spawn, but these runs are so depressed

thanks to the eight (count 'em, eight!) dams they must traverse to and from the sea, that I haven't bothered to try and chase them for several years. But that doesn't mean I haven't learned from the times I have gone steelhead fishing.

The most important lesson? The spey cast isn't just for rod-wielding anglers. In fact, my friend Simon Gawesworth, the brand ambassador for RIO Products, uses the spey cast on my local rivers here in eastern Idaho. He's become quite evangelical about spey casting. RIO has even introduced a single-handed spey fly line for traditional anglers who don't use spey rods, but who can incorporate the spey cast into their repertoire.

Is it difficult? Yes, at first, particularly for new anglers. But if you know how to roll cast and mend, spey casting will soon become very intuitive, and it's a cast you should have in your repertoire.

In time, you'll learn to identify the "point" in your cast—the target, which is usually downstream and across at about a 45-degree angle. You'll learn how to make the right "D loop" behind you when you load your cast, and you'll learn how to avoid the "collision loop," which happens when you improperly load your cast.

And, if you're like a lot of anglers out there, the spey cast becomes so intuitive that you might one day find yourself using it more than a traditional fly cast. —**CH**

22. Give Yourself a "D"

The best letter grade you can give yourself in fly casting—particularly roll casting and spey casting—is a perfect "D." Simon Gawesworth is one of the best casters I've ever fished

with, period, and he literally wrote the book on spey casting. But it doesn't matter if you're throwing a big two-hander Skagit style, or roll casting a little 4 weight on a brook, he says the shape you want to form on that backcast (start with the rod tip low to generate surface tension and load the rod) is a "D." As you raise that rod tip to fire forward and uncork the cast, the line behind you should look like that perfect arc of the letter D, extending from the water surface on the bottom to the tip of your rod up top.

If you practice a lot at making D shapes, you will improve those casts dramatically. And if you're losing it, and frustrated, odds are, you aren't making a good enough D. I was once on the Dean in British Columbia with my friend Andrew Bennett, and I had for some reason lost my groove. He politely came over and tapped me on my shoulder, then showed me a quick video he had just taken of me with his phone. I was too eager on the forward stroke, and the more frustrated I got, the worse I cast.

He reminded me to let that D form up, and with one, simple adjustment, I was back in the game. You don't have eyes in the back of your head either, so sometimes a video assist from your fishing partner can help a lot. —**KD**

23. **For Goodness Sake, Stretch Your Line (Every Time)**

There is no more clear demonstration of angling stupidity than to watch someone cast the rod they've had sitting in their base-ment for eight months, only to come up woefully short on the cast . . . and then listen to them suggest that their $800 rod isn't cutting the mustard. I can say this, because I've had many moments worthy of nomination to the "Darwin Award fly fishing hall of fame" myself. Granted, it's human nature. You see those trout rising, or the tarpon rolling, and you want to get right down to business!

But trying to cast a line that's been wrapped tightly on a reel is like trying to shoot a corkscrew through a drinking straw. Finally, after years of embarrassing myself, I've embraced the notion of stretching my fly line before I even think about looking at the fish and the water. It's a ritual now, every time I fish, and even if I fished that rod and line the day before. Have your fishing partner grab the end and pull. Half-hitch it around your trailer hitch and pull. You don't need to stretch the whole line; try forty, fifty, sixty feet for starters. You should also dress it and clean it, but that might be a bridge too far for most (in all honesty, including myself). Just straighten it. All the good tips we've offered on casting and zeroing in on fish

won't matter for beans if you don't have a straight, slick line to work with in the first place. —**KD**

24. **Listen to Jack and Clean Your Line**

Jack Dennis is a good friend and mentor, and he was a very close friend of Charlie Meyers. He's one of those guys who probably really has forgotten more about fly fishing than any of us will ever learn in the first place. But one of his best casting tips is also a gear tip, and one of the simplest things we can do but only about 2 percent of us are actually smart enough to do it frequently (and I'm not one of them). Clean your line. All the time. With dish soap, warm water, and a towel. Why? Because casting a fancy expensive rod with a worn-old line is like driving a race car with flat tires. —**KD**

25. **Quick Casts for the Flats**

When I chased bonefish for the first time, I was an absolute mess. I had a shabby double haul, a clumsy approach, and a game built for a trout stream. It was awful.

But, of all my faults, my friend Rod Hamilton, an expert flats fisher from British Columbia, pointed out that my worst fault was my tendency to false cast too many times and then lay out a cast that was often too late.

He gave me some advice on that first trip to the Bahamas that I've used many times since, and I've used it with great success.

Rather than depend on my reel so much, Rod suggested that I let out a good eighty feet of fly line, and let it trail behind me. Then, with my off hand, I could hold my fly between my thumb and forefinger (taking care to make sure the hook point is down—failing to do this once resulted in me driving a Size 6 Pink Puff deep into the meat of my forefinger when my rod tip nailed a dive-bombing gull on my backcast).

Then, when I saw cruising fish, I could toss the fly up, make a single backcast to load the rod, and send as much line as I needed toward the bonefish. No false cast. No wasted motion.

It's easily the best advice I've ever gotten about flats fishing (not including the "Don't trout-set!" admonition I got from my fishing onlookers when I missed my first real chance at a bonefish on Long Island in the Bahamas years ago). —**CH**

26. A Great Reach Cast Is Worth 1,000 Mends

I think "mending" the line is so important that I honestly wish anglers would spend as much time practicing mending—lifting and placing the fly line upstream of the flies themselves, so as to mitigate drag—as much as they practice casting itself. Seriously, I don't care how you get it there, what matters after the flies hit the water matters *far* more than the delivery.

That said, if you can make that mend in the air, before the fly or flies even hit the water, you are so much better off than you would be tinkering around after everything lands.

The reach cast is probably the most important fish-catching cast any fly angler can hope to master. Simply put, it entails making the normal cast, extending the line and leader over the target, and then at the very end, you make a semi-subtle move to reach across your body so that the fly line lands upstream of the fly or flies.

Say you are fishing a run where the current is moving from your left to right. You're a right-handed caster. Make your normal cast, but at the end, softly bring the rod back toward your face, and touch your left ear. See how the flies and line land. You're in business. Reverse all that from the other side or if you are a lefty. It's not rocket science, but you must master reach casting if you want to take things to another level. —**KD**

27. **Challenge Your Cast**

The great casting instructor John Juracek asks that we all remember that when it comes to the most important aspect of fly fishing—casting—knowledge does not equal behavior. We actually have to go through the motions of casting, time and again, before we achieve competency. So grab your rod—or your practice rod—and make a few strokes. Keep in mind that all progress takes place outside the comfort zone . . . so challenge yourself. It's fun. —**CH**

28. **Rig for the Roll**

We talk about "bow-and-arrow" casts and all that, and knowing how to fling, flick, and otherwise present a fly when the overhand cast isn't feasible. That all makes perfect sense to me.

What doesn't make perfect sense in this regard is that we'd ask a 5-weight rod we use for casting across open currents to do those specialty casts in tight quarters on a narrow stream.

My favorite place to fish is a narrow spring creek that has gin-clear water and lots of brush.

When I go there, I have a special rig: a six- and one-half-foot fiberglass, flexible 3-weight rod. But I think a short, specialized leader is the most important part of the rig. I rig 4X to the fly line, then chop it down, and go 5X, maybe 6X (never less) in quick succession. That total leader length is never more than six feet long. But I always have at least two feet of the thinnest diameter tippet leading the fly. It helps to rig your leader in a way that reflects the casts that you anticipate making 90 percent of the time, and in that place, I'm rolling 90 percent of the time. —**KD**

29. **Over-Lining Is Overrated**

So someone told you, somewhere along the line, that to get extra "oomph" out of your cast, you might consider "over-lining," meaning, putting a 6-weight line on your 5-weight rod, and so on, and so forth.

Before you do that, you should know that all the line companies are already a step ahead of you. They know all about what it takes to load the fast action rods. For example, a RIO Gold line is already really weighted one half more than what's being billed (a 5 weight, for example is really a 5.5 weight) and a RIO Grand is already a full line weight above the number on the box. Not faulting RIO by any stretch, they're just marketing lines that actually load easier, with more feel, on the types of rods they know people are buying. And that's the same for Scientific Anglers and all the other line companies. In other words, they're already factoring in all your faults and foibles, just to make you feel better about the casts you make with your fast-action rods.

If you really want to dial your casting stroke, you'll embrace a medium-action rod, and match it with an honest line. And if you're going to stick with that fast-action rod, feeling the weight of the line, so you can start and stop the rod tip effectively can and should happen without over-lining. —**KD**

30. **Use the Water to Load the Rod**

So much attention is paid to casting fancy loops overhead, forming the perfect wind-cutting "U" shape, and all that . . . which is wonderful. But your best friend for setting up a great cast is the water right in front of you. Friction and resistance built up by pulling and lifting a fly line off the water is the best rod-loader in the world. Keep that tip low when you start the backcast, and half your concerns are taken care of. If you try to do everything in the air only, you'll only spook fish. Too many false casts, too many adjustments, only hurt you! You want to strive to be a "pick it up and set it down" caster. One shot, baby, matters most, and that's true whether you're banging mangroves in salt, or pounding the banks with hoppers on a trout river. Done right, a one-shot, water-loaded cast can and should travel up to sixty feet or more, which is plenty range to catch any trout, tarpon, bonefish, permit, carp . . . or any other species. —**KD**

PART TWO

Reading Water (and Fish)

31. Fly-Fishing Jazz

Some of the favorite writing I have ever done was for Marshall Cutchin and Midcurrent.com. Those pieces still exist in the *Midcurrent* archives, and I humbly encourage you to check them out online. But there is a backstory (there's always a backstory) that led me to connect fly fishing with jazz music, and I still very much embrace it to this day.

I come from a very musical family, and I have loved music since I could walk. I initially wanted to be a drummer, like my father. But I didn't practice nearly enough, and when I went to try out for the seventh-grade band, I got cut. But rather than quitting, I took an alternate path. I literally went off to school on the bus one morning with a pair of drumsticks in my hip

pocket, failed miserably in the audition, and came home on the bus toting a bulky case with a rented tenor saxophone.

It was the best musical turn of my life. Because instead of just quitting on music, I resolved to learn the new instrument. And it turns out that there is no sexier, no more captivating instrument than the tenor sax. I found *notes*, beyond the beat! So I poured myself into the sax, and my folks were super-supportive. They signed me up for lessons, and things took off from there.

Reading Water (and Fish)

By the time I was thirteen, while most of my friends were jamming pop and rock music, I was in my bedroom with a turntable, spinning vinyl albums and trying to emulate artists like John Coltrane, Gato Barbieri, and Lester Young. (This is all true!) Even stranger, my parents took me as a young teen to concerts and clubs, and I saw icons like Sonny Rollins and Stan Getz. Later, in college, the best date I ever remember was taking my girlfriend (now wife) to the "Bird of Paradise" club in Ann Arbor to see Dizzy Gillespie. I was weird on jazz, and still am. She still tolerates all this.

Transposing to fly fishing, which I took up at the same time I was dating my (now) wife, I immediately connected fly fishing with jazz music. The simplest way to explain it is to say that you have to learn certain fundamentals if you want to go anywhere. The fundamentals, which are sometimes boring, tedious, uninspiring things such as basic jazz scales, and perfecting your embouchure, and finger positions . . . or, in the fly-fishing world, learning to hone your casting stroke at the "10 and 2" positions on the imaginary clockface, timing, and subtly double hauling, feeling the rod load, learning how to make a drag-free drift of a fly . . . are absolute prerequisites to stepping off into the "artisan" realm of either. One must practice, practice, and practice, to the point where tedium becomes muscle memory.

If you do that, you give yourself the keys to the kingdom of *improvisation*. And fly fishing, like jazz music, is ultimately about the ability to improvise. You play off the basic scales and techniques you learned and practiced, but you take everything to your own level, and apply that to the moment. You very rarely play the same solo—with a fly rod or a musical instrument—the exact same way. And that is the true wonder of fly fishing . . . and jazz music.

I have many friends who are far more disciplined and regimented than I am, and they are fine anglers. Almost by definition, we anglers try to "pattern" things, and script everything out, and it's almost like trying to play a Mozart concerto or a Puccini opera note for note. And that works for some, so I'm not discouraging that.

But when I hit the river, the soundtrack in my head is almost always Coltrane, or Charlie Parker, or Chet Baker. I have great confidence that I know the scales, the timing, and the fundamentals, but with that in mind, I'm *always* playing *off* the sheet music, constantly pushing boundaries and improvising, with purpose and direction.

So I encourage you to endeavor to be a "jazz" artist as you fish. Master the fundamentals. Understand performance. And then riff, improvise, and follow your soul. Even if you've never picked up a musical instrument in your life, if you follow this pattern of thinking as you approach your fishing, you'll find your own sweet melody, and that's where the greatest rewards are ultimately realized. —**KD**

32. A Swirl or a Rise? Know the Difference

There's a difference between a swirl near the surface and a full-on rise when trout are feeding. Being able to tell the difference could mean the difference between success and failure.

A swirl or an "eat" just below the water's surface means the trout are likely eating emerging insects, not full-on duns or adult midges. You can tell a swirl when the water moves, but doesn't necessarily involve the jaws or the head of the fish leaving the water. Sometimes a good, healthy swirl results in a heart-stopping tail slap on the water as the eating trout pushes back into deeper water.

Fishing to swirls involves emerger patterns that drift just under the water's surface. Or, as I've taken to doing lately, it can involve fishing soft-hackles on the swing. Craig Mathews of Blue Ribbon Flies in West Yellowstone, Montana, has converted me into a soft-hackle junkie on waters like the Firehole and the Madison, where emerging flies are often incorrectly imitated by dry-fly anglers with full-on mayfly duns. The bonus to swinging soft-hackle? Trout will sip a dry fly. They'll absolutely hammer a soft-hackle making its way up the water column on the swing.

A rise might be easier to identify, particularly in softer water. Here, you'll get the patented rise ring, and the fish, rather than diving after eating, will tend to fall back into their feeding lane, awaiting the next meal. This is when a match-the-hatch dry fly is most effective. —**CH**

33. Eating Places

The fact is that most fish, especially trout in a river, have eating places and holding or hiding places. Recognizing those different places is an important thing, but the most important lesson is that you do not want to get into the habit of casting

☆ Eating Spots
✖ Hiding Spots

flies into holding, and especially hiding, places. Fish don't eat there. They don't like breakfast in bed. Eating places are where foam lines form, where fast current meets slow, the sweeping reverse eddy, even the little washboard ripple. Cast there and leave the hiding spots alone. —**KD**

34. Go "Back to School" on Small Streams

Growing up fishing the small streams of Colorado's high country, I managed to acquire a lot of innate fly-fishing skills that have translated to just about every fishing situation I've encountered over the years. Chasing wild trout in small water is still my favorite fly-fishing "discipline," and I credit small streams with educating me about everything from simple

entomology and trout biology to reading the water to a more disciplined approach to casting.

A lot of people turn up their noses at fishing small water, assuming, often incorrectly, that small streams are full of small fish. They choose instead to chase fish in bigger water, under the assumption that it's more challenging and that the likelihood of catching trophy trout is greater. I would offer a counter assumption: If you can read water on a small stream, you can do the same on bigger rivers, only with an eye that might be a bit more fine-tuned. If you can cast to a spot on the small stream, you can do the same on bigger water. If you can cast undercover, or roll cast to fish on a small stream, those skills translate.

A small trout stream is simply a big trout river in sharper focus. Learning—and continuing to hone your skills—on small water only serves to make you a better angler, regardless of where you fish and what fish you're after. Learning the "short game," if you will, only serves to sharpen individual skills that you can put to use on a larger scale. For instance, learning a compact roll cast beneath a low canopy on a small stream will certainly help you make a better cast when you're in a driftboat, tight to the bank, in search of a big brown that's hiding under an overhanging cottonwood branch.

For a lot of small-stream fishing, the cast is compact and tight. Wasted movement, like a big arch in your backcast, often translates into flies caught in branches. Small-stream fishing is, by and large, an economic form of angling. Casts are usually shorter. Targets are smaller. Demands on things like accuracy and presentation are more acute.

Small streams are great places to freshen up your cast, hone your water-reading ability, and craft ways to approach fishing in a way that allows you to best cover water, move through a day on the water and, more important, catch more fish. Think of small streams as little trout universities, where you have the chance to build on your fundamentals and earn your degrees of expertise that you'll apply to more "advanced" fishing situations later. —**CH**

35. **The Fish on the Pillow**

Now the fish on the pillow, or cushion, riding right in front of the rock in the current is always a fair target. The pillow is a hydraulic cushion on the upstream side of a large rock in the stream. It literally allows a fish to ride there without exerting much energy. It certainly isn't much of a hiding place, but it is a holding place. And it is an eating place. Sometimes a trout will ride that cushion for ease but will definitely be looking for food as she or he does so. This is the fish that I sweep a streamer fly in front of as a first option, casting from upstream at or near a 45-degree angle. I'll dangle a dry after that. Maybe I'll try to swing a nymph also, but I don't try to hit the pillow rider from downstream with a nymph rig. They're either going to play or not, usually within two casts, and more often than not on a streamer pattern. —**KD**

36. **Go Vertical**

Trout move horizontally in a run; upstream, downstream, and the like. But the fish that you are casting at is most likely to transition vertically, and you need to play your fly selection and presentations accordingly. For example, the trout is munching away happily in a run, and you show it your Size 16 Pale Morning Dun. It looks, but doesn't commit. What next?

Wait a minute or so and show the fish another PMD (you had its interest in the first place) but size down to a #18. This time, the fish shows similar enthusiasm, yet still doesn't commit. What next? Wait a few minutes, tie on a #18 PMD Barr Emerger, and make that cast. No takers; stop, wait, and go lower, this time with a #18 soft-hackle pheasant tail, with a bead. Do this *even if* you see that fish tip its snout up to take a natural dry fly. You take your game deeper, go vertical. Don't futz around with twenty different dry patterns on the top. That fish knows something is going on, and it's going to retreat farther and farther into the safety zone, which means going deeper. Play that vertical game, and you might win. Stay only in the horizontal game, and sure, you might find the magic pattern, but that might realistically require several minutes between patterns and casts, and most of us, including myself, don't have that patience, and besides, we might run out of time. If you're on the clock with a challenging fish, I'd play the vertical game before I diddle around with twenty options on the surface. —**KD**

37. Shade Is Cover, Too

When structure is lacking, consider casting along the "shade line," or where the shadow from stream- or lake-side structure falls on the water. Often, trout and other predators will lie in

the shadows where they're less visible to overhead predators while they wait for food to come to them. Casting right along the shade line can prove deadly, no matter what fish you're after, or what kind of fly you're using. —**CH**

38. **The Smartest SOB in the River**

Age, size, and genetics all factor into a trout's "intelligence." Admittedly, intelligence is a relative term because no matter how old, big, or native a trout is, its brain is most usually the size of a smallish nut, so "smart trout" is kind of an oxymoron.

That said, when an angler endeavors to fool a trout, what she or he is really doing is matching wits with instinct, and a native trout that is descended from ancestors that have inhabited its waters for thousands of years is literally a different animal than the fish-farmed triploid that was dumped in the river last week. Those "Disneyland" fish make for interesting photos, and they are fun. Don't get me wrong, I enjoy catching them as much as anyone, and I'm not afraid to admit it. But wild fish are better and native fish are best.

In fairness, if you're willing and able to make a strenuous hike way into the western high country to find native cutties in a stream, or bushwhack into a pond in Maine that doesn't see a lot of pressure, the fish you'll find there, willing to chomp down on simple patterns like Royal Wulffs and Trudes all day long aren't exactly "intellectual giants," because they're not used to human influence. Which is great, and a sign that unpressured trout are way more predatory by instinct than we give them credit for. For example, you can go to Kamchatka and lob a mouse fly into the middle of a spring creek, and watch five- and six-pound trout charge like waking missiles toward the fly—and your whole perspective on the predatory instincts of rainbow trout will change forever.

In my book, the "smartest" fish are the wild fish. Fish that are descended from populations that have been there for about a hundred years or so . . . large enough to have been around the block a few times, pressured just enough to have an edge to them. It sounds almost silly to say, but that's why carp are the newfound challenge fish for many anglers, and for me, it's why the wild brown trout in places like Michigan, Montana, New Zealand, and beyond are special in their own right. Fish for wild browns long enough and you will swear they can smell you, see you, feel you, and force you to bring the top-level game every time you chase them. —**KD**

39. **Hidden Structure**

On my favorite little cutthroat streams in eastern Idaho, there's a small gorge where the stream runs fairly straight. Apart from a couple of small, rapid sections, the stream, at first blush, appears devoid of structure. It's not—the structure is just hidden beneath the water.

When you come to a stretch of water that you think might be devoid of fish because nothing is giving you clues otherwise, get out of the river or stream and find some elevation. Look for subsurface rocks that you might not be able to see from river level, or hidden drowned logs that have settled to the bottom. It might be just a rock the size of a softball, but if it breaks up the consistency of the current, fish will hold behind it. Consider, too, inflowing spring seeps, shade lines, and foam lines. I've pulled really nice fish from water others walk by, simply because they assume the lack of obvious structure means there's no place for trout to hold. Slow down. Take a look. You might be missing some great fishing. —**CH**

40. **The Keys to Spotting Fish**

The more you fish, be that on rivers, on saltwater flats, beaver ponds, wherever, you learn that sightfishing is the real drug. If you can see them, and then trick them, that's top of the game. It doesn't matter if you trick them with a nymph in a river or a

Crazy Charlie on a saltwater flat (or an ugly ol' carp in the golf course pond, for that matter). At least for me, sight fishing is the juice. And I think, if we want to be totally honest about it, that's the core reason why people travel great distances to cast at trout in New Zealand, or stalk bonefish on the flats in the Bahamas or Belize, whatever. I just think one gets to the point where they've felt enough tugs, and then they want to see *why* that happens. And they'll trade twenty blind tugs for just one "see 'em, trick 'em, hook 'em, fight 'em . . . let 'em go" scenario.

Many of the folks I now fish with ask, "How did you see that fish?"

I'd tell you that I have TSP—trout sensory perception—or supernatural skills, but that would be a lie. Heck, I can't read the face of my watch, or tie on a fly any more, without the help of reading glasses. But at trout- or bonefish-spotting range, thank goodness, I'm still as keen with my eyes as my bird dog is with her nose. There's really no secret to any of that. It just boils down to six things.

First, you need to fish enough to recognize the things that are not a fish. Process of elimination is the benchmark. Get rid of the weed mats, the twigs stirring in currents, and the shadows that don't actually move, and you are halfway home.

Second, I never look at an entire flat or run in a river. I imagine I'm looking through a screen door, and I eliminate all possibilities through that screen, then virtually lift and place that screen door to another piece of water. One chunk of water, maybe three by seven feet at time.

Third, I'm never looking for a whole fish. If I see a whole fish, great, I'll certainly operate off that and cast accordingly. But I'm really looking for pieces of fish—a tail slash, a dark spot moving, a subtle color change that doesn't exactly match up with the water.

Fourth, I wait for motion. If I'm staring at a shape or shadow that does exactly the same thing, over and over, I become skeptical. A live fish is going to offer variance from the pattern, sooner or later.

Fifth, I try to think like a fish. Where would I go, and what would I eat, and why? The best fish-spotters understand fish behavior, and they look where they think they are most likely to see fish. Literally focus on "fishy" places (depth changes, color changes, foam lines, riffles, current changes, etc.) and you'll likely see more fish. Profound, I know . . .

And sixth, I wear good polarized glasses, and I switch lenses based on what the natural light conditions are. Amber or copper might be my baseline on a trout river, but on a cloudy day, I wear yellow or blue lenses. On a very bright day, I wear mirrored lenses. I don't mean to sound like a salesman for the sunglass companies, but I always have at least three different tints in my boat, and I even carry different alternative tints in my pack when I am walk-wading. Any given day I fish, I switch back and forth an average of three or four times, depending on what the clouds and sunlight are doing. —**KD**

41. The Foam Line Is Good for Fish . . . and Anglers

I've heard the "foam is home" phrase a lot, and I'm betting most avid fly anglers have too. There's a reason for that. Foam lines provide several benefits to trout that are likely well-known—foam provides cover and it often traps emerging bugs, making it a buffet line of sorts for feeding fish.

But foam is good for anglers, too, because it shows you exactly how fast the current is moving, and gives you a really good clue about where to cast, how much line to mend, and how fast to strip if you're using a streamer.

Yes, foam is home to fish. But for intuitive anglers, foam offers up hints that, too often, we don't heed. —**CH**

42. **Take Your Punishment**

The true appeal of fly fishing in New Zealand is that there is no place in the world where the angler is more richly rewarded when he/she does everything perfectly, and more harshly punished when he/she does not. Apply that to your thinking, on your home river. Accept and embrace the humility. Know

that will make you a better angler. Learn from it. Adapt. Don't bring the same approaches, the same script you read online or through books or magazine articles, with you every single day to the same river to fish for the same trout. Be big enough to take your punishment, adapt, and adjust. That's how you become a better angler. I cannot count on my two hands the times I was absolutely humiliated by those wonderful resourceful fish I so desperately wished to catch. But I learned . . . and I took the lessons to heart . . . and I made subtle changes, and eventually won. Punishment is a good thing. Learn from it. Embrace it. And turn it in your favor. —**KD**

43. **The Retrieve: What Fly Are You Using?**

Too often, anglers who fish streamers or subsurface flies (or poppers and gurglers!), particularly in salt water, have what I call a "default" retrieve. It's their go-to retrieve for flies they have to bring to life in order to entice a strike. Instead of asking yourself "How fast should I strip?," ask yourself "What fly am I using?" That should give you the information you need to know to make your inanimate streamer, baitfish pattern, shrimp, or crab imitation look more lifelike.

Using a baitfish pattern, like a Clouser? Ask yourself how baitfish swim. Better yet, ask yourself how a baitfish in distress might swim. A quick strip followed by a pause and then maybe a couple more strips. How about a shrimp pattern, like Schminnow? A quick burst followed by a pause, perhaps? A crab imitation? Try a slow retrieve that keeps the fly deep and right where a crab is supposed to be. A crawfish pattern—my favorite late-spring carp fly? Crawl it along the bottom, but occasionally give it a quick strip, particularly if you see it attracting interest.

Topwater stuff? You want them to like a food source in distress. You want them to attract attention and move water. Quick strips. Rod wiggles. Whatever it takes.

It's not about how fast or how long you strip. It's about what you're fishing with . . . and what you're fishing for. —**CH**

44. **Chase the Alpha**

Floating down the East Branch of the Delaware River in New York, the great guide (seriously, still one of my top five anywhere, and will remain such) Joe DeMalderis on the sticks, and none other than Tom Rosenbauer (Orvis) in the tailgunner' seat.

But I'm up front. And we see heads working. And fair or unfair, it's really all on me.

Still, we're a team at that point, and the first thing Joe did was slow the boat down. I cannot remember now if he just dropped anchor or he was pulling hard on the oars. But we stopped dead straight about fifteen yards above a pod of feeding fish in an eddy. And, as the guy in the bow, I could tell right away who "Big Daddy" was. Three or four slurpers and sliders in the run, but only one big "toilet flush" gulper eating his lunch in the bottom of the run.

It was a Hendrickson hatch, and we probably could've caught some of those tattlers also. But Joe said we were going "all in," and as such I tied a Hendrickson emerger pattern on my tippet. One fish . . . one shot . . . one cast. No questions, no playing around . . . do or die.

I made that cast. I caught that fish—a hefty four-pounder at least. Even Rosenbauer, who has caught many better fish in tougher circumstances, would attest to this one, I am quite sure.

The lesson is very simple. If you see a dream fish, and you know in your soul you want to catch *that* fish . . . load up, make a great cast and catch that fish. But before you can do that, you need to make an educated decision to forgo any other fish in the pod, and you need to make that fish an offer he/she cannot refuse . . . on the first drift over its head. And if you have any doubts in your mind whatsoever, you should make that fly an emerger (or a cripple pattern). Don't be throwing several variations the people at the fly shop told you might work. You lose mojo every darn time you cast a fly, no matter how beautiful the drift might be. For a big trout, working with purpose, hit the best fish with the best bug, right then. All business. Get right to the point. —**KD**

45. Fish Where It Gets Dirty

Often, trout and other predators will hang out in the transition zone where dirty water meets clean water. A good example of this is on the Green River in northern Utah, where Red Creek comes into the river's famed B Section. After a rain—even just a sprinkle, honestly—Red Creek dumps a load of dirty, reddish water into the Green, creating a noticeable "transition zone" between clean and dirty water. Often, the fish will hang out in this zone and wait for the food being delivered to them from Red Creek.

I had a similar experience on Lago Yelcho in Chile several years back, where a glacial creek gushed into the lake. Yelcho's massive lake-dwelling browns would hang out right where the tinted glacier water met the deep, green water of the lake and wait for food to come from them.

Look for inlets and confluences where so-called dirty water comes into clean water. This is fishy habitat, and predators will take advantage of it. —**CH**

46. Thermal Refuges

Much like looking for where stained water meets clean water, look for areas in a river or creek where cooler water meets warmer water, particularly if you're fishing for trout in the summer, when warmer water tends to push fish into "thermal refuges."

Here in Idaho, on my favorite cutthroat trout stream, I've hooked some of my best fish where cold spring water flows into the main stem of the creek. Even water just a few degrees cooler serves as a trout magnet when it's hot outside.

Look, too, for spring seeps and telltale vegetation like watercress—this plant is an indicator of the colder, cleaner water that trout need to survive and thrive. —**CH**

47. Weed Beds Warm Up Earlier

Several summers ago, I took my son to northern Manitoba to chase toothy northern pike on the fly. It was early in the season, the first week of June. In the days prior to our arrival, the weather had been stellar . . . sunny and warm and just perfect.

Of course, by the time we arrived, the weather turned, and we found ourselves fishing for a few days in cold wind and sideways rain, sometimes enhanced with little ice pellets that really put a sting in the sometimes-gale-force wind.

But we found fish, largely because the guides, members of the native First Nation Cree community, knew where the pike would be, even in sketchy weather.

For the most part, we fished over the previous season's decaying weed beds.

Why? Decaying plant matter gives off heat, and even the subtle temperature difference between the open water of the lake and the shallower water over the weeds—perhaps just a degree or two—was enough to attract hungry pike.

When we finally got some sun, we fished all manner of fishy habitat: rocks, shoals, grassy banks, and the like. But when the weather turned sour, the guides looked for old weed beds and the warmer water hovering above them. —**CH**

48. **ID the "Player" and Get After It**

You are told that if you want to get the maximum out of a run, you start at the back and work your way from downstream to upstream, picking off the trailers first, and then the alpha fish

in the sweet spot. But do you know how often that script really works? About once in one hundred tries. If I can see the fish in a run, I go right for the big one, or the pretty one, or whatever I decide to be priority number one, right away. Of course, if you spook other fish to get to your main target, that hurts your chances. But devise plan A from the onset and execute. —**KD**

49. **What Are the Birds After?**

Often, hatching insects are difficult to identify, either because there are very few of them, or they are very small. I spend a lot of time in Yellowstone National Park, and there may not be a better trout river than the Firehole when the park opens to fishing the last Saturday in May.

And, often, the bug that's hatching—a very small baetis mayfly, or a Blue-winged Olive—is so hard to imitate because of its size that many anglers don't recognize the hatch. On the Firehole —and this is true on most trout rivers, particularly freestoners with very predictable hatch patterns—I tend to watch the mud swallows to determine what's hatching and just how prolific the hatch really is, given that, at certain times of the day, it's tough to see tiny bugs like the early (and late) season BWOs.

If the swallows are plentiful, and it's late May or late October, I can, with great confidence, assume that the Size 22 (or even Size 24) baetis hatch is happening. I can then choose my fly (and hopefully find a twelve-year-old nearby to help me and my aging eyes tie it to my tippet!).

Birds are telltale creatures to the fly fisher. Always keep an eye to the sky to see what they're doing. This is likely even more important for saltwater anglers—terns and gulls will crash bait that's been pushed to the surface by predators underneath, and, often, those predators are what we're after as fly anglers—think striped bass, speckled trout, bluefish, and the like. Some of the best fishing I've had in salt water has been done by simply following the birds and casting where they're feeding.

Thankfully, for the most part, they don't mind sharing. —**CH**

50. **Potholes for Winter Redfish**

Several years ago, I spent a chilly December day with Capt. Danny Wray in marshes behind Grand Isle, Louisiana, prospecting for the region's winter redfish. Unlike the area around

Venice, Louisiana, Grand Isle doesn't get the big "bull red" run in the winter—instead, it sees smaller reds from the Gulf of Mexico slide into the marsh in search of warmer water (shallow water warms faster under the sun).

A couple of good fishing buddies from Montana and I were in New Orleans for an unrelated event, and we decided to spend a day fishing away from the city. We drove a couple of hours to Grand Isle, climbed into some kayaks and, despite temperatures in the low 40s, had a great day fishing to redfish.

The secret on such a cold day? The marsh is pocked with bathtub-sized depressions where reds would congregate in the warmest of the marsh waters. If we found these holes, we'd find fish. We didn't see fish tailing or chasing bait in the shallows, but, in terms of sheer numbers, it might have been my best redfish day ever.

It also helped to have a guide who knew what to look for and wasn't afraid to share it with a handful of western trout guys. —**CH**

51. The More Changes the Better

Okay—and I beat this drum too much, says my buddy Tim Romano—but fish like changes. Doesn't matter if you're shark fishing off California, or trout fishing in the Smoky Mountains—fish like changes in currents, changes in depth, changes in water color, and changes in structure. If I see a place where a few changes are happening at once—a hard seam on a shelf, indicated by a change of water color, where the current swirls around some rocks—that's where my first cast lands. —**KD**

52. **Elevate**

Often, a bird's-eye view of the water will reveal the secrets of a run; many times, even a fish. This is much easier accomplished when you're fishing with a guide who can get above the water, perhaps on a bluff or even in a nearby tree. We've all seen photos of guides perched precariously above the river, pointing at an angler in the water and telling him or her where to cast.

But you can do it yourself, too. For instance, there's a great run on Idaho's Salmon River, and above it perches an old ponderosa pine stump. Years ago the tree fell over the highway and construction crews had to clean up the mess, leaving the stump behind.

That stump makes for the perfect viewing platform for finding migrating steelhead in the river below. More than once, I've stood on that stump and stared into the clear waters of the river in search of finning fish. And more than once, I've found one, moved down to the river, and made a few casts. I've even managed to catch a couple.

From elevation, you can get rid of many limiting factors when it comes to spotting fish, especially the glare off the water you'll often deal with at river level.

My favorite example of this? Several years back, I was staying in a high-rise condo on the beach in Destin, Florida; I was enjoying my morning coffee on the patio overlooking the Gulf of Mexico from eight floors up. Down the beach about a quarter of a mile, I noticed a bait ball moving slowly up the beach, right in the first trough of that gentle gulf surf break. Every now and then, I'd see the bait ball—probably Atlantic bunker—froth and foam as jacks and speckled trout picked off stragglers.

Quickly, I grabbed my 7-weight, hopped in the elevator, and arrived at the beach just as the bait moved right in front of

my condo. For the next hour, I enjoyed some great fishing, all because, from elevation, I could see what was happening in the water below me.

You don't have to be eight floors up, obviously, but by finding some high ground, you can see things you just can't see from water level. —CH

53. That Fish Is Really Upstream of the Rings

A quick little reminder (perhaps statement of the obvious) but I'll make it because I'm sometimes guilty of making casts at the rise rings I see on the surface of a moving river. Even if it's a slowly meandering spring creek, that fish actually rose and ate

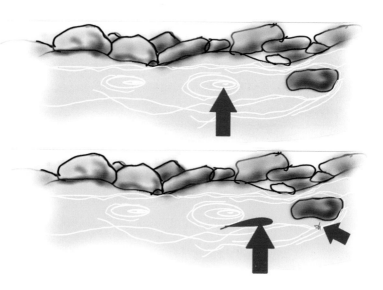

the bug a couple feet above where you spot, process, and cast to where you think it was. I once wore scuba gear and watched my friend cast at the fish that was merrily sipping bugs about six feet away from me. Every cast landed on its tail. Exasperated, I surfaced, and asked what was going on. "I'm landing it right in the middle of the rings, like a bull's-eye!" my friend said. "Yeah, but the fish is actually making those rings about two feet farther upstream." —**KD**

54. **Hovering Fish and "Hoovering" Fish**

I find this true especially with carp, but you can also apply it to trout in many places. You can often pick your fly by reading the body language of the fish you are after. If you see them hovering just below the water surface, they're looking up

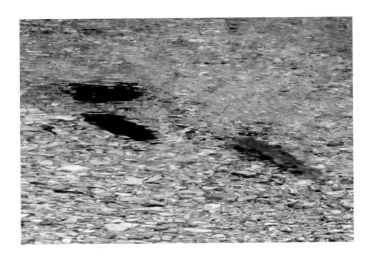

and are ripe for the dry fly or the emerger. The "Hoover" fish vacuuming the bottom needs to be shown a crayfish, nymph, worm, or egg. If you throw dry flies at the vacuum cleaner, no dice; if you hit the suspended fish with a bottom bug, that won't work either. —**KD**

55. **Carp and Mud**

Once, while fishing from a skiff off Beaver Island in Lake Michigan with carp gurus Steve Martinez and JP Lipton, we came upon a school of hundreds of ten-pound-plus fish. But we couldn't really see the fish shapes—the water was a little milky and they were a few feet deep. What we could see was the

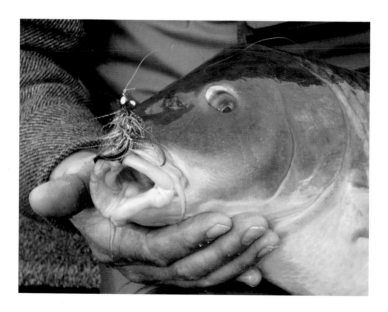

mud cloud behind them as they fed. It was like a herd of buffalo kicking up dust on the plains. All we had to do was drop our casts a few feet above where the mud trail started, and we were on a carp festival the likes of which I haven't seen since. Watch the mud—for carp or for schooling bonefish on the flats. If the front edge is moving, that means a chow line. —**KD**

56. **Plan the Fight**

If you aren't at least thinking about what happens after you hook a fish, knowing where it's likely going and what you'll do to counter that, you're making a mistake. Every run or flat I look at, I ask myself two questions: Where do I think the fish are now, and where are they going to go when I tie into them? —**KD**

57. **Rob the Slow Banks**

Many of us are conditioned to fish the side of the river with the most structure—as in, from a driftboat floating downstream, we tend to fish along the bank with riprap rocks, fallen trees, and such. That's a smart play for most of the year. But not in the early season, when the runoff is just starting to come down, the water is still cold, and the currents are pushing. The riprap bank collects all that debris because the water is so turbid. Fish don't like to eat there. Instead, in the early season, I'm always going the opposite direction and fishing the soft, slow banks—maybe the grassy shoulders or the little riffles off the island. Water you wouldn't expect to hold much is exactly where the fish are in the early season. Once everything settles

out and stabilizes, then you can go back to the dominant bank. But I think (water) speed kills the odds of good takes in the early season. —**KD**

58. Carp Talk to Each Other

You might have heard that carp release pheromones in the water when they are spooked, and other carp pick up on that stimulus and react in kind. So if you spook one fish, you often spook them all. It's not like trout, where you can pick fish up from the back of a run, and so long as they don't thrash the whole run, you can pick more up as you work upstream. Off Beaver Island, Michigan, I saw an odd phenomenon repeat itself over and over. Fishing with Kevin Morlock, we saw a lone carp cruise up onto the flat. Kevin told me to hold off, and the carp cruised away. A minute or so later, the same fish came back, but this time it had a handful of friends swimming behind. We let them all cruise off, and sure enough, a few minutes later the "sentry" fish came gliding back up the flat, and this time it brought the whole school of dozens of carp with it. I swear carp can talk to each other. Keep that in mind if you see carp cruising up on shallows from the deep. Often if you let one go, it will be back with friends. —**KD**

PART THREE

Flies

59. The Greatest "Hatch-Matching" Story Ever Told

Tim Romano and I once enjoyed a brilliant week of fly fishing for goliath sea-run brown trout from the legendary Kau Tapen Lodge on the Rio Grande in Tierra del Fuego, Argentina. It was a surreal experience to be standing in the iron-gray currents of the Rio Grande, with the wind buffeting across the stark, austral landscape, casting two-handed rods as you're being watched by guanacos (like small llamas) and condors. And the take by a fresh sea-run brown is sheer thunder.

As always, the greatest "catches" of the week were the friendships forged with other anglers of like spirit—in that case, those who have literally traveled the world to dally with trout.

I wrote this about one of them for *Field & Stream*: "Lilla Rowcliffe may well have the greatest fishing stories I have ever heard. She's easily among the most intrepid anglers I have ever met. She has traveled from England to many parts of the world to chase fish with flies, including taimen in Mongolia, mahseer in India, and Atlantic salmon throughout Europe (she's holding a photo of a beast she landed on the River Spey some years ago). To say Rowcliffe has 'game' is an understatement. She's out-fishing me at around a ten-to-one clip at the moment (she's had her guide piggyback her across the river to get in the best spot to cast). But I am not alone. Several years ago, she set a remarkable benchmark at Kau Tapen by landing over six hundred pounds of sea-run trout in one week, with the average fish being thirteen pounds. I should probably also mention that she is eighty-seven years old.

"I asked her why women are often naturally better anglers than men. It's true, after all. Rowcliffe agreed and shared an anecdote that a certain angling expert, befuddled by female prowess on the water, once theorized that women have a pheromone effect that attracts fish. He believed this so much that he took to carrying his wife's undergarments in his pack as he cast.

"What men often don't understand is that fishing is not about power," she said. "A woman will feel the fish take, and her natural instinct is to do exactly the right thing at the moment . . . let the fish go."

Women may indeed be better hatch-matchers than men, but I know for sure that Ms. Rowcliffe had the best "hatch-matching" story I've ever heard.

She related her story from the River Cauvery in India. Having caught the mighty mahseer, she and her guides shifted attention to tricking carnatic carp. Though they saw rises and whorls, none of the fishing guides could dial in on the exact pattern to toss. Then one morning Rowcliffe woke to find monkeys jumping about in a banyan tree overhanging the river.

"I noticed one monkey dropping poo in the river, and up popped this carp right there. I thought 'Lilla at last you know the secret!' As I knew what monkey poo looked like (apparently gray and round), I found a Muddler Minnow in my fly box and, still in my pajamas, I went out to fish. On the second cast, I caught one. I ended up catching seven that morning and thought, now at last, I am a proper fly angler, because I know how to truly match the hatch," she said. (The story is another example, by the way, of how the muddler may indeed be the most versatile fly in the world.)

Some years later, the tale made its way into an angling book of some note in the U.K. When her daughter described the episode to a ghillie at the Scottish fly shop she stopped at to buy a copy of the book, he exclaimed: "My goodness, I did not know your mum was the monkey s*** lady!"

Romano and I remember Rowcliffe for far more than that. —**KD**

60. **UV Resin in Home-Tied Flies**

Consider using UV-reactive resins in the bulk of your home-tied fly patterns—even dry flies. This may seem like overkill, but UV resins come in various viscosities, dry quickly, and really help improve a fly's durability, even if your whip finish or half-hitch might be a little weak.

Some UV finishes are so thin—they're no more invasive than traditional head cement—and with a bath of UV light, they dry immediately, hard as nails, to protect your knots and your flies so they fish longer and last longer.

As a bonus, there are brands of UV resins that are environmentally inert, meaning you're not going to be doing any undue harm to the environment or yourself when you're tying flies. Additionally, some companies are starting to make dyed resins that can help make streamers and nymphs even more appealing. —**CH**

61. **Multipurpose Flies**

Years ago, I was much more of a "pure" fly fisher. Dry flies were for upstream presentations only. Nymphs were for dead drifting. Using either fly in any other fashion was . . . well, not pure.

These days, when I'm on my favorite cutthroat streams here in Idaho, I've become a much more pragmatic angler. That's not to say I still don't appreciate that slow dry-fly sip of a native cutthroat, but I've taken to going with flies that might be fished different ways, even on the same cast.

For instance, a Stimulator is a great attractor that can represent anything from an adult salmonfly to a grasshopper, particularly on the dead drift over likely runs. But it's also a great skater that can mimic a dancing caddis or, in larger sizes, even a small mouse. Armed with enough flotant and desiccant, flies like the Stimmy, a Royal Wulff, or Trude pattern can allow you to offer different presentations to fish in the same stretch of water, and on a single cast.

Don't let old-school "purism" get in the way of catching fish. You're still fly fishing, after all. —**CH**

62. **Black Posts One Direction, White the Other**

Pete Cardinal on the Missouri in Montana is one of my favorite guides in the world, and one of the smartest anglers I know. We had a chance to reconnect a few years ago and fish a nice *Baetis* hatch. It wasn't a very complicated affair—the trout were on Parachute Adams, #18, and all it took was a good cast and decent

drift to earn an eat. But it was later in the day, and the sinking sun made for a funky glare. One direction was Technicolor clear, the other a silvery haze. No problem. Pete simply carries the same patterns with two different colored posts— white for casting with the sun

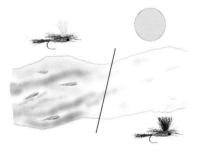

behind you, and black for casting in the glare. It all looks the same to the trout from underneath. But you can see white posts better in one direction and black posts better the other, all depending on where the sun and the glare are. I now carry black and white variants of the same staple patterns of classic dry flies—like Adams, PMDs, Green, Brown, and Gray Drakes— even ants and beetles, for that very reason, and that has made life a lot easier—**KD**

63. **Sparse for Salt Water**

My friend Frank Smethurst once critiqued my saltwater fly-tying efforts as "too bulky and too colorful." At the time, I was doing my best to imitate the little "sardina" baitfish that school off the beaches of Baja California's East Cape, where they're often pursued by big jack crevalle and roosterfish. After all, out of the water, sardina are a bright bluish green, so I tried to imitate that color with blue tinsel and green craft fur.

It was overkill. In the water, the sardina are a flat brownish-gray. And they're very lean. Over the years, after fishing more in salt water, I came to realize that saltwater flies, such as Clousers and the like, don't need to be very beefy. Tie them sparsely. As my friend and fellow angler Mike Sepelak says, "When you think they're sparse enough, take some more out of the pattern." —**CH**

64. **"Unmatching" the Hatch**

Sight fishing and brown trout are two of my favorite things in the world, and when you put the two together, that's hard to beat. Perhaps no community of anglers (except maybe the Kiwis) is more tuned in to this phenomenon than the fly fishers in Tasmania, Australia. After all, Tassie is where the very first browns were expatriated from Europe, and were it not for Tassie browns, there might not be browns in New Zealand, or the United States, Argentina, and so forth. And Tasmanian anglers have been "polaroiding" for their beloved brown trout for about a century.

Guide Daniel Hackett of Riverfly 1864 out of Launceston gave me a cool tip one afternoon when we were locked in on a

hefty specimen of *Salmo trutta* that was happily munching away on mayfly duns. "Sometimes, it's as important to *un*-match the hatch as it is to match what the fish are eating almost exactly."

Now, as an angler who had spent his whole life being told that the "holy grail" for the fly angler was to be able to notice exactly what insects were hatching, and the trout were eating—and then be able to reach into a carefully prepared box of flies and pull out and tie on a nearly perfect facsimile—well, Daniel's thought almost seemed like blasphemy.

But as he explained further, it all came into focus. Give them something that looks close to the naturals but seems *just a little bit meatier*, and the trout might go for that over all the other bugs that look exactly the same. Give them something that you the angler can see better, so you are more apt to react appropriately to a strike, and your odds go up. Give them something that looks more vulnerable and the fish will probably choose that fly over something it has to earn with more effort.

As he talked, I started thinking about some of the things my guide friends had taught me as I was writing my first fly-fishing book, *Castwork*, over twenty years ago. Dan Stein on the Bighorn taught me to tie on a #14 Blue Dun during a blanket midge hatch. It looked nothing like the teeny little midges (who wants to mess with a #28 pattern anyway?) but it caused the naturals to cluster on it, creating a veritable "meatball" of insects that trout couldn't refuse. Pete Cardinal on the Missouri taught me to throw a fuzzy H&L Variant during a Trico hatch, because it looked close enough to the menu, but I could see those white wings from forty feet away. Bob Lamm on the Henry's Fork—or more exactly on the Madison arm of Hebgen Lake as we were chasing "gulpers" with *Callibaetis* patterns—insisted that we throw cripple patterns, because they simulated bugs that couldn't quite shed their shucks, and as such were easy pickings for the trout.

Turns out that in the most technical, yet often most interesting and rewarding, dry-fly scenarios, I had already been taught to "un-match" the hatch to kick my game up to a higher level. And that works no matter where you go to chase smart trout, anywhere in the world.

So you should consider doing the same. Absolutely endeavor to do your ready best to notice what the fish are keyed in on, and match it as close as you possibly can. But then dig just a little bit deeper in your mind, and in your fly box, and try to find something that's just a tad different, just a bit off-kilter and unique that will set you apart from everything else those fish might have seen from other anglers who stocked up at the local fly shop. And when you do so, be thinking about three things—what the fish would rather eat, what you can see, and what looks like easy pickings. Dial that in, and your dry-fly game goes up a few notches. —**KD**

65. UV Parachute Posts

Tying parachute patterns isn't really all that difficult, and the benefits of parachute flies are many; they can be mistaken for both upright duns and spinners, and, perhaps most important, they're easy to see for us anglers, particularly if your eyes are anywhere as bad as mine have become over the years.

But parachute posts can sometimes be tricky. My friend Tim Flagler, who does a video series on fly tying that we try and promote often on the Trout Unlimited blog, showed me a great method for tying parachute posts, and it's so simple that it spurred a full-on face-palm and a "Why didn't I think of that?" moment when I first saw him do it.

Rather than tie in the post and spend time wrapping thread ahead of the post, behind the post, and around the post, consider using a sparse length of Antron fibers, tied directly to the hook shank where the post belongs. Lift the post upright, make a couple of wraps with tying thread in front of the post, and then twist the post counterclockwise with your left hand while your thread hangs off the shank. Then, take the smallest amount of UV resin and apply it to the base of the post. Dose the treated post with UV light and, voilà! An upright parachute post that's ready for hackle.

Was I right? Why didn't we think of that!? —**CH**

66. **Tip the Fly for Tying Parachute Posts**

Yes, the UV resin tip is a solid one, but for some flies, just that bit of resin adds just enough weight to sink the fly altogether. So here's another idea I got from Tim Flagler: tip the fly in the vise.

In other words, after you tie in the post material—calf tail, Antron yarn, whatever—tip the fly in the jaws of your tying vise so the hook point is facing down. Then, to craft your parachute post, simply wrap the post material vertically. This also makes it easier to tie in your hackle—wrapping vertically is a more natural motion for most of us who tie our own flies, so this method just *feels* better. And the results are excellent. —**CH**

67. The Miracle of the "Mole Fly"

The *Baetis* (blue-winged olive) hatch is one of my favorites. Thing is, with BWOs, trout can be ultra-finicky. You can throw a Size 18 pattern, get refused, and then switch to a Size 20 (you should always size *down* on a refusal) and get refused again.

Jon Easdon of Angler's Covey in Colorado Springs showed me this trick. He told me that when the chips are really down, and we can't figure out how to make it happen, we pull out this fly.

Now, admittedly, the Mole fly isn't sexy. You might, in fact, wonder what all the buzz is about.

It has a CDC wing, a brownish rabbit fur dubbed body, and not much more. It was invented by Charlie Craven, whom I

think is easily one of the most innovative and effective fly tiers in the world. It stands in a column of bugs in a feeding lane. But part of it sinks to the vulnerable level. The profile is perfect.

It's hard to maintain this bug and keep it floating. One cannot simply dab flotant on it and let it ride. The secret is to keep a chamois cloth to dry things out and use specialized CDC dressing from the start. Dry that bug as much as you can between casts, and go from there.

What I will tell you is that I have used this fly from the best BWO waters, everywhere from the Delaware to the Henry's Fork, and nothing, but nothing, earns a bite like this fly. When the chips are down, when you've tried every other bug in the box, try this one, and if the fish won't eat it, move on. They won't eat anything you show them. —**KD**

68. Caddis: The Most Dishonest Fly Ever

We all love caddis flies. I think that's because caddis hatches are so prolific on our favorite rivers. The famed "Mother's Day" caddis hatch on the Arkansas in Colorado is rivaled by the clouds of caddis that show up in late spring and early summer on rivers like the Madison and Big Hole. Caddis can hatch anytime from spring into fall. I've seen caddis hatches during snow squalls in November on the Henry's Fork. I've seen caddis hatches take place in the Sag River above the Arctic Circle in Alaska to the Yelcho River in Chile and almost anywhere in between.

But my friend Tom Rosenbauer, while discussing the importance of caddis flies as trout food, explained to me that caddis flies are "the most dishonest fly ever."

Why?

Because adult caddis flies actually spend very little time on the water, where they are available to trout. The good old Elk Hair Caddis pattern might be a dependable trout slayer, but Rosenbauer, who's worked for Orvis for more than forty years, offers some really good advice when fishing caddis patterns.

Avoid the typical mature caddis patterns. Instead, he says, go with patterns that represent emerging adults and "cripples" or, even better, fish more caddis nymphs. Once they "hatch" from the water, caddis flies only return to the water to lay eggs—they dance and flit around, spending the bulk of their time hovering above the surface, not in it.

I put the theory to the test on the Rio Chimehuin in Argentina's northern Patagonia region one December afternoon. Caddis were everywhere, and there were rising fish going after them. It took me about an hour to realize that the fish that were actually rising to the mature caddis pattern I was using were actually pretty small. When I switched to an emerging caddis pattern—one that rested a bit deeper in the surface film—I started catching bigger trout.

The logic makes sense. Larger, more experienced trout aren't likely to waste the energy needed to pursue a "maybe" meal that a mature caddis offers. Instead, they're going to put their energy into meals with more promise—emerging bugs or bugs that are trapped in the surface film (cripples). I caught even more fish with a cripple as my lead fly, and an unweighted caddis nymph as a trailer, about two feet below the cripple.

"Dishonest" might be the wrong word. But, I'm a believer that a mature caddis pattern fools as many anglers as it does trout. Consider using cripples, emergers, and even nymphs the next time you find yourself in a cloud of busy caddis flies. —**CH**

69. **Wire or Tinsel for Dry Flies**

Using anything with weight to tie dry flies seems counterintuitive, but sometimes the smallest addition of shiny brass wire can really dress up a dry fly and make it more durable. I sometimes use very small brass wire to segment the body of bigger dry-fly patterns, particularly foam flies that float well. This keeps the foam together longer, and can help keep palmered hackle in place, too.

Also, my favorite Stimulator pattern incorporates a gold 3D tinsel—this little bit of sparkle not only makes the fly more visible to fish, but the shine off the material sometimes helps me see the fly better, too.

To compensate, I might go a bit heavy on the flotant, or dose the fly in desiccant more often, just to make sure it floats better and longer. —**CH**

70. **The "Pellet Fly" You Can Feel Good About**

We've all likely stood at the lip of a fish hatchery raceway and watched as several thousand fingerling rainbows boiled to the surface in pursuit of fish food in the form of pellets. In waters that are stocked with these hatchery-reared, laboratory-crafted "rainbow" trout, flies that resemble this fish food can be killers.

But, let's be honest. If we wanted to catch cookie-cutter trout on pellets, why would we get into fly fishing at all? Why learn about entomology? Why worry about fly size, profile, and presentation?

Hand-feeding a bunch of clones is not why we fly fish.

But there is a "pellet" fly you can feel good about and, as is the case throughout just about any discipline, competition spurs innovation. The Perdigon Nymph (and all of its adaptations) has been embraced by the competitive fly-fishing community because it's absolutely deadly for trout—and Perdigon is Spanish for "pellet."

No, not the kind of pellet you buy by the handful and dish out to the kids to feed the hatchery fish. "Pellet," in this instance, references firearms, not fish hatcheries. Perdigons are tied slender and heavy, and they cut through the water much like a hunk of lead . . . or a pellet from a shotgun or an airgun.

The Perdigon Nymph, developed and fished by competitive fly fishers in Spain and France, is a sinking nymph, usually coated in a thin film of UV resin and fished deep, often bounced off the bottom by Euro-nymphers and high-stickers. It catches fish. It wins fly-fishing competitions.

Now, not all of us are into fly fishing for the competitive aspect of it. Most of us just enjoy fishing . . . and catching fish. The Perdigon helps with the latter. Learn something from the pros and carry a few deep-riding Perdigons in your nymph box. —**CH**

71. **Practice, Practice, Practice**

I've become adept at the tying vise (and I use that word not because I'm gifted, but because, with time and practice, I can be, as Garrison Keillor was fond of saying, "above average") when it comes to a handful of patterns. I can tie a Stimulator in my sleep. Same thing with a Parachute Adams or a Shminnow or . . . well, a good handful.

But I do try to stay sharp at the vise by expanding my tying repertoire. I'll never be a Charlie Craven or Bob Clouser. Never. But I spend time every couple of weeks watching Charlie's tying videos (and the videos produced by others in the "vise squad," like Tim Flagler and Matt Callies). Their craftsmanship while tying flies inspires me to pick up a new pattern now and then and tie up a dozen. Often, the results are predictable—the first couple look like something the cat coughed up and the last couple look fairly serviceable . . . worthy of sticking into the fly box without worrying that my fishing buddies will ridicule me for my ineptitude.

The point is, it's important to stay sharp at the vise if you enjoy tying at all (if you don't, you don't—I get it, and there's no judgment on my end). Tying any pattern, from giant articulated pike protein to a Size 24 Zebra Midge, will hone that tying muscle memory and make it easier to pick up new patterns, tie them proficiently, and eventually put them to use on the water.

Just like any discipline within the larger fly-fishing craft, practice is vital. —**CH**

72. **Peacock Herl . . . and Why It Works**

Many classic fly patterns have one common ingredient— peacock herl. There are lots of theories for why this venerable material works so well, but the best one comes from my friend Mick McCorcle, an angler from Fredericksburg, Texas.

"As a former biology nerd, I have a couple of microscopes I sometimes use to view natural specimens," McCorcle explained. "One cold winter day, I pulled out some peacock herl and began to examine it under increasingly higher magnification. At each level, the herl was iridescent. As the magnification got higher, the field of view got smaller, but the iridescence was still evident. No matter how high the magnification, the iridescence never dulled."

Perhaps the best evidence for using peacock herl? Fish really seem to like the way it looks. Most fish, trout included, have both rod cells and cone cells in their retinas (for both scotopic and photopic vision), and their eyes have a spherical lens. Many fish are also sensitive to UV and polarized light. Mick's note that the peacock herl has an iredescence is spot-on—it's also UV reactive.

Some of the best flies tied with peacock herl? The Royal Coachman and Royal Wulff are two classic patterns, but just about any traditional nymph pattern can be tied with a herl collar, and I've taken to using herl wraps on a lot of my traditional dry flies, like Stimulators and even caddis patterns. The Griffith's Gnat is a good example of a small midge cluster tied with herl.

The lesson? Peacock herl is a versatile attractor material, and fish dig it. That's good enough for me. —**CH**

73. **Let Your Beads Oxidize**

I'm all for bead-head flies, because I like how they sink. But I'm not keen on bright shiny new beads. Some people think that the bead looks to a fish like an air bubble. And others might

argue that the twinkle of a bead reflecting sunlight works like a spinning lure. I think both of those theories are corny. A shiny lure is supposed to look like a shiny minnow, and I've never seen an air bubble that looks like a brass bead. The beads are for weight, and weight sinks nymph flies fast. I like patterns with beads hidden in the thorax section of the bug, specifically because it hides the weight better. Failing that, I like to leave my bead flies sitting out in the weather, sun, and open air for some time before I use them. You have to mind the hooks because you don't want them rusting, but in my mind a tarnished bead makes a fly a little stealthier and more ready to fish. —**KD**

74. **Tying Articulated Streamers**

Whether you're tying full-on articulated "meat whistles" or just tying streamers with trailing "stinger" hooks, the secret isn't in knots or, depending on the type of fish you're after, in the material you use to connect the main body of the fly to trailing section. The secret is in the tying itself. In fact, good articulated patterns aren't tied using knots at all.

Over the years, I've watched other vise-monkeys like me offer different methods for tying the lead hook to the trailing hook, or the body of the fly using articulated fly shanks to the stinger hook, and I'm convinced that I've finally stumbled upon the easiest method.

First, as I mentioned, it's not about a knot. Instead, treat the material you're using to connect the trailing hook just like any other material you might tie into a fly pattern. With your hook connected to your trailing line (I'll get to the material shortly), simply place the line atop the lead hook or shank and tie it down, starting at the bend in the hook and working your way to toward the hook eye.

Next, stretch the leftover material toward the bend, and tie back to the original tie-in point. This is where I like to dose the entire stretch of tied-in material with either a thin coat of head cement or, even better, a coat of very thin UV-activated resin. Splash the coating with a UV light and you've got yourself a virtually unbreakable connection between your lead shank and your trailing hook.

As for the line between the lead and the trailer, consider your target. For trout and bass, a nice segment of heavy mono (fifteen-pound test or better) should work. For toothy critters, like pike, barracuda or bluefish, consider something different, like a stretch of thirty-, forty-, or fifty-pound Spiderwire.

And you have some options here. You can go with a single stretch of line, tied to the trailing hook eye in a somewhat traditional method, or you can choose to attach the trailing hook by looping the material through the hook eye and tying both ends of the material to the lead hook shank. Both work, but I prefer the latter, because I think it adds to the strength of the fly, both by providing two lengths of line to the trailing hook, and by giving it two attachments to the lead shank. Honestly, though, it's a preference thing.

As for length, consider two things:

- The length of the material that stretches behind the lead hook or shank, like the marabou or the stretch of rabbit or bucktail . . . or whatever;
- And, whatever you choose to attach to the trailing hook, if anything at all (obviously, a stinger hook will be bare, and shouldn't extend past the tail material tied to the lead shank) should cover the hook so it blends nicely with the material from the lead shank.

You can also double the durability of the fly by choosing to lash the trailing material to the trailing hook, much like you did to the lead hook. Rather than loop the material to the trailing hook eye, stretch it a bit farther down the shank and tie it in. Then, dose it with cement or resin. This adds more strength to the finished product, and for most angling situations, stronger is so much better.

No, it's not rocket science. It's actually a fairly easy method for crafting good articulated patterns, and for those who've spent time trying to use the knot method, this might seem overly simple. Give it a try and see if you don't like the outcome. I know I like not tying knots which often break over time. —**CH**

75. **My Starting Lineup Now**

I absolutely believe that a fly angler can make a lifetime of memories by fishing ten patterns well, and ten years ago, when Charlie Meyers and I published *The Little Red Book of*

Fly Fishing, we tossed out ten staple patterns. I still believe in those patterns with all my heart. But now, ten years later, with over one million miles traveled, I'd refine that list just a tad. The twelve flies I have in my box now, no matter where I am in the world (to fish trout), are:

Charlie Craven's Mole Fly Size 18

Pat Dorsey's Mercury RS2 #20

Jack Dennis's Amy's Ant # 12

John Barr's Beadhead Copper John #16

Tim Heng's Autumn Splendor Streamer #8

Parachute Adams #14

Tungsten bead, soft-hackle Pheasant Tail nymph #14 (or #16)

Don Puterbaugh's Caddis #14

Mike Mercer's Missing Link Caddis #16

Dave Whitlock's Whit's Hopper #10

Jay Zimmerman's Backstabber #8 (best carp fly in the world, but under-appreciated for big crawfish eating browns)

Gold-Ribbed Hare's Ear #14

There are a zillion other cool bugs, and great variations, to be sure. But trust me, you can travel the world, and fish in any local season, and catch fish anywhere if you carry these patterns in your box. I've been travelling and fishing for decades, and these are the patterns that have caught me the most fish, throughout the world. —**KD**

76. Wood Duck Fibers for Mayfly Nymph Tails

Years of subscribing to online video fly-tying channels have helped me hone my tying, and I've picked up lots of great tips from many renowned tiers. But this one is maybe the simplest: Wood duck fibers look almost exactly like the tail fibers found on many natural mayfly nymphs. Consider using a half-dozen or so wood duck fibers when you're tying nymphs meant to imitate mayflies—the Pheasant Tail nymph is an excellent example. —**CH**

77. Cutting Foam and Rubber at an Angle

Working with foam and with rubber (think rubber legs) can be tough at the vise—both tend to jump around and they can be hard to anchor to the hook. In addition to having a nice thread base for friction between the material and the hook, consider cutting both materials at an angle and attaching the angled piece of the material to the hook. You'll find it much easier to tie onto the hook and much less likely to spin or jump as you're tightening your wraps. —**CH**

78. Eyes for the Prize

Ever since 2008, when I first fished for dorado in the jungle rivers in Bolivia, I've been a big believer in barbell eyes on all my streamer patterns. I even put little barbell eyes on little black

Woolly Buggers. Maybe that's just quirky, but unless the fly is absolutely meant to imitate something else like a leech (which a Woolly Bugger certainly does sometimes), I like to give my streamers eyes. Not evil Eye of Sauron eyes . . . panicked, please don't eat me eyes. Of course, maybe the weight factor is as important or more than the aesthetics. But it's a more interesting story to say the eyes draw the predator. I believe that 100 percent for dorado. If the eyes fell off, or the paint got scuffed off, the fish wouldn't eat it, and that fly was useless. —**KD**

79. **Cord Your Thread for Tough Material**

Some material is just hard to tie into fly patterns. I've always had issues with deer hair—it likes to spin on me and jump up the hook shank when I'm tying, often leaving me so frustrated that it takes *two* tumblers of Jameson to get me through an evening tying Muddler Minnows.

The solution? Spin your bobbin counterclockwise and cord up your tying thread. This accomplishes two things. First, as you go to tie in your deer hair, foam, or whatever material is giving you fits at the time, the thread will jump back toward the bend in the hook and back atop your material. Second, the corded thread, as it tries to unwind, offers more friction between the thread and the material.

The converse is also true. When you want a sleek fly body, uncord your thread with a clockwise turn. This flattens the thread out and allows it to cover more space on the shank or atop your secured fly materials. —**CH**

80. **Big Bugs, Little Bugs, and Just-Right Bugs**

My good friend Dave Kinney related a cool story from Penn's Creek the other day. He had a few things going on at once. First, an epic Sulphur hatch . . . also some BWOs. . . and then some Green Drakes appeared on the water also. Ten years ago I would have told him to go with a Green Drake pattern. After all that's a bigger bug—more protein for the punch, right? Maybe not. Maybe a Sulphur because they were the most abundant, so they had the fish's attention more. That didn't work either. We'll never really know if one bug species actually tastes better for trout than others, but I think it comes down to the stage of the insect, and its vulnerability, most of all. Turns out the mayfly spinner fall was the ticket, and there is no more lethal pattern when there are both duns and spinners in the mix. I call rusty spinners the "Goldilocks" fly because many times I have been on the river with multiple bugs hatching and/or falling—this pattern is too hot. . . this one too cold. . . but ol' rusty, more times than not, is *just right*. —**KD**

81. Cut Hair at an Angle

While we're talking about tying in clumps of hair—deer hair or elk hair, in particular—here's a great tip from Tim Flagler, renowned vise guy from New Jersey. Cut the butts of the hair at an angle, and lay the hair atop the hook. Then, as you're wrapping the hair—with corded thread!—you'll catch just a few pieces of hair with each wrap until you've managed to secure the whole clump. The result is a solid wrap and you'll find that the angle prevents a big bump in your fly pattern. This makes it easier to tie other materials in over the hair. —**CH**

82. It Isn't Always About Protein (but It Often Is)

Sure, you want to "make it a meal" sometimes, but if fish only ate flies based on how much "food" they got for the effort, we'd throw nothing other than giant leeches and mouse flies all day, every day. Sometimes, the fish go with what's most abundant and comfortable, which is why a nondescript little zebra midge works so well. Sometimes, as is the case with anadromous fish like Atlantic and Pacific salmon that aren't really "eating" when they bite a fly, all you really want to do is agitate. Knowing when to open the buffet, versus setting out a small appetizer, versus ticking a fish off is a big part of fly selection, especially when there aren't tons of naturals on the water to tip you off. —**KD**

83. **Know Your Bucktail**

The hair fibers on a full bucktail may all look generally alike, but they aren't. Proficient tiers use hairs from different locations on the tail to accomplish different things. For instance, the hairs near the tip of the bucktail are very cooperative when tying them atop a hook shank. They don't try to shed the thread, and they lay down nicely. These fibers are perfect for patterns like Clousers and Deceivers.

The hairs at the base of a bucktail are a little tougher to work with. They flare dramatically when they're tied in, just as normal deer hair might. These fibers are good for spun-hair patterns and bass bugs. The hairs in between? They're the "happy medium" on any bucktail. They flare a bit when tied in, but not as dramatically as the fibers near the base. These middle-section fibers are good for bullet-head patterns and such.

A single bucktail might be the most versatile fly-tying material you have on your table right now. You just need to know how to use all of it. —CH

84. Replace Vise Jaws Yearly

Do you tie flies? A lot? If so, you've probably noticed that the vise's grip tends to get softer and softer over time. Nothing is more frustrating than trying to seat a whip-finished knot, only to have the hook move in the vise or come completely free.

Renowned tier Charlie Craven recommends that, for those of us with good, expensive vises, we replace the vise jaws at least once a year. It's good advice for avid tiers and will more than pay for itself in overall finished-product quality. —CH

85. Profiles and Silhouettes

In terrestrial season, I carry and fish two colors of flies: black and tan. I think it's all about profile, size, silhouette, and (especially with the case of rubber legs) action. In soft light and medium light, I fish black patterns like classic Chernobyl ants, and in the stark bright light of midday, I fish tan Amy's Ants. I used to think a hopper fly wasn't any good unless it had a red tail, but I do not think that anymore. I think it's almost entirely about the size and shape of terrestrials. I could be wrong. Wouldn't be the first time. —**KD**

86. Less Material, Faster Sink

Build big streamers with as little material as you can possibly get away with. You don't want a bulky streamer tied with excess "stuff" for two reasons. First, the more material on the fly, the harder it is to cast effectively once it's wet and heavy. Second, more material actually serves as resistance under water, slowing the sink rate for streamers. Trust me. Less is better. —**CH**

87. What Dr. Behnke Told Us About Colors

I know many of you who have heard me speak, or read what I've written elsewhere, will be familiar with this, but it's worth saying again. When I first took over as editor of *Trout* magazine, I inherited the column of the late Dr. Robert Behnke, who was the teacher (Colorado State) for so many fish biologists and such, and the preeminent source of trout biology information for many of us in the media who needed things explained to us. To get to work on a column for the magazine the last couple years of his life was an honor.

One could write volumes on trout, flies, colors, and such, but I'll try to boil down what an expert fly angler needs to know in several short bullets.

- Trout do see colors, and they respond better to the blue-violet side of the spectrum than the red-orange side. That makes sense, because red turns to gray and is the first color to lose its character as it travels deeper in water. Any photo-taking scuba diver will tell you that.
- If a hatch is on, you want to be as close to the exact color as you can.
- That said, profile and size are probably more important than exactly matching color—hence the century of effectiveness (and counting) for the Parachute Adams.
- If no hatch is happening, and you're prospecting or using "attractor" patterns, that's where the purples and blues come in . . . hence the popularity of the purple Prince Nymph, the natural likeness of which you will never find, under any river, anywhere in the world.

When it comes to other fish, like tarpon, and throwing roaches or bunnies at them—purple or tan? Chartreuse or red? That almost entirely depends on the water clarity and sunlight, and most of all, what you feel good about throwing. —**KD**

88. **Bigger Scissors for Tying Flies**

Let's face it. Perception is reality. And most perceive fly tying to be a precision craft that requires small, laser-sharpened cutting implements with uber-fine points. But precision doesn't have to be accomplished using the tiniest tools, particularly when it comes to scissors. Of late, I've taken to using larger scissors in my tying, mostly because the smaller tools are uncomfortable—I'm getting older and I'm prone to some mild arthritis in my fingers and thumbs. Larger scissors can still have fine points and razor-sharp edges, and be easier to use thanks to larger finger holes and longer blades. Are you experiencing more cramps in your fingers when you tie? Or maybe you're getting those telltale indentations on your fingers or thumbs from smaller tools? Try a set of larger scissors and see if it doesn't help. —**CH**

89. **The Woolly Bugger—Not Just a Streamer**

The venerable Woolly Bugger is likely the first fly those new to tying make at the vise, and I don't know any anglers who don't have 'Buggers in their fly boxes. Many have entire boxes dedicated solely to the tried-and-true streamer.

But the Woolly Bugger is so much more than a streamer, and anglers who understand how to fish this fly will have more success with it. I love fishing 'Buggers as the point fly under an indicator, particularly if it's got some weight to it. In darker colors—from brown or olive to jet black—the fly is a service-able imitation of a stonefly nymph, and its weight will help get a smaller or trailing nymph down into the strike zone, giving you more chances to hook trout.

I've also used 'Buggers under indicators in still water; a weighted Woolly Bugger, lightly jigged in still waters where leeches or worms are present, can be a deadly pattern for cruising trout or bass. No doubt about it, the 'Bugger is among the most versatile flies out there, and anglers should fish it more often. —**CH**

90. **Use a Point Fly During a Midge Hatch**

If you're like me, and your eyesight isn't magically improving over time, fishing to rising trout during a midge hatch can be frustrating. Picking out a Size 22 Griffith's Gnat among a host of natural midge clusters is a hopeless endeavor for me. So, I've taken to fishing two dry-fly patterns during really prolific midge hatches—one is the "target" fly, the other is a larger attractor, or a "point" fly, usually something like a Size 14 Parachute Adams.

When fish are keyed in on midges, the bigger point fly likely won't attract attention (but sometimes, it does!), and that's okay. I tie the tiny cluster pattern about eighteen inches below the point fly. This gives me two points of reference: first, I find the point fly and know that, generally speaking, the target fly is riding downstream from it and that I can often follow the general path and see my cluster pattern on the water. Second, if the light is low or I just can't find my cluster among the naturals, I know about where it should be, and any rise or strike in the general neighborhood earns a hook set.

It's not foolproof, but it does increase my catch rate significantly during a midge hatch. And, with such small flies, it doesn't impede my cast and doesn't make my fishing any more difficult than it might be if I were to only cast the Size 22 gnat. —**CH**

91. **Weighty Eyes Matter on the Flats**

When you are chasing ultra-wary bonefish and permit on the flats, a loud "plop" when your fly lands often spells doom, even if you make a cast to the perfect spot. The shallower the water, the less of a splash you want to make. Naturally, in deeper water, you can not only get away with a heavier fly, you need more weight to get the fly to sink. As a rule of thumb I don't carry thirty or more different fly patterns; I carry about ten different fly patterns (usually a mix of small shrimp and crab imitations) but I have three or four different varieties of each, ranging from heavy dumbbell eyes to lighter bead chain eyes to no dumbbells or beads at all. The fish will tell you if you're making too much commotion. If you see them run away from a good cast, size down in weight right then. It isn't the pattern that turned them off, it was the plop. This all holds true on the carp flat on the river, lake, or pond close to home also. —**KD**

Flies

92. My Favorite Carp Flies Are Bonefish Flies

Carp are famous for adapting to a specific food source: They eat berries that fall off bushes in the creeks and canals around Washington, D.C.; they zero in on small fish like gobies at places like Beaver Island, Lake Michigan; and pretty much anywhere there are crayfish, you can't go wrong with a great Jay Zimmerman fly pattern. But I've found that some of my most effective carp flies are bonefish flies like Gotchas, Pink Puffs, and Crazy Charlies. I think, like on the saltwater flats, it's really more a matter of presentation and not spooking the fish you are targeting than it is matching the forage. As I said before, the weight of the fly (the splash factor) is as important a consideration as any. Having those different patterns with various weighted eyes—from heavy barbells to bead chain to nothing at all—is as important to me when I'm on the carp flat as anything. That is unless, of course, I know they're on one of those specific food sources like berries or gobies. —**KD**

93. Except When My Favorite Carp Fly Is a Trout Fly

Then again, if you asked me what fly I have probably landed the most carp on overall, it would be a Size 12 or 14 beadhead Hare's Ear with rubber legs. Small, slow micro strips with that bug will fool even the smartest old carp. —**KD**

94. Sparse for Permit

Anglers have a natural tendency to want to make their flies look as "beefy" as possible, and that can be a problem. I do it all the time myself, asking "why not make it a meal?" and assuming that a permit, for example, is twice as likely to eat a big old crab pattern than it would a stringy little shrimpy thing. But if you think about trout fishing, you know the best thing to do on an obvious dry-fly refusal is to size *down* with your pattern. I've found that many of the permit I've caught have eaten smallish shrimp patterns—and that's usually because I was really looking for bonefish and that black sickle fin of a permit just happened to swim into view. With no time for a wholesale switch, I just went with what I had. Permit eat good presentations. The fly pattern is not usually the deciding factor. That said, I have, over the years, become a firm believer in the "less is more" approach—from thin bodies on pheasant tail nymphs for trout to sparser and whispier flies for bonefish and permit. —**KD**

95. The More Chewed-On Your Hopper Flies Are, the Better They Work

Another mistake it took me years to get over was the assumption that if a fly isn't in perfect condition, it won't work very well. Nothing could be further from the truth. Give me, for example, a Whit's hopper that's been chewed on, looks tattered, even ragged, but still floats with a dab of grease, and that's worth its weight in gold on any Michigan or Montana river in late summer in my book. I wouldn't trade one properly chewed-up hopper fly for ten new ones from the fly bin. (And for the record, let me say that the fishing world knows no finer gentleman than Mr. Dave Whitlock, who invented the Whit's hopper . . . and Dave's hopper . . . and . . .) —**KD**

96. **March to the Different Drummer**

We all know that local guides have favorite patterns with good reason. If you're lucky enough to fish with Brian Kozminski in northern Michigan, or Coz Costolnick on the Delaware, or Amy Hazel on the Deschutes in Oregon, you can bet your bottom dollar that they'll have a "home remedy" in their kit that works like a charm. But I've found that one of the benefits of my travels has been taking patterns from one area of the country and applying them to others. For example, Amy Hazel was kind enough to hook me up with a box of her favorite steelhead flies from Oregon, which I took home to Michigan with great effect. One of the hottest bugs I fish on the Colorado River, near where I now live, is a hairy dun pattern tied by my friend Daniel Hackett in Tasmania, Australia. And I'm not showing a photo of it, because I don't want anyone knocking it off and fishing it! I like being the only person in Colorado fishing that bug to fish that see thousands of patterns, many of them the same, over and over. Sometimes "marching to the beat of a different drummer" in the spirit of Henry David Thoreau is all it takes when it comes to fly selection. —**KD**

PART FOUR

Presentation

97. The Enlightened Trout Angler's "Grand Slam"

To advance your overall game, you should be proficient in all aspects of fly fishing, and not get stuck in only one way of fishing. A perfect "grand slam" day for me has become less about different species caught, and more about different methods used. If I can catch fish on a dry fly, a nymph, and a streamer in the same day, that's the best fun. I'm done quibbling with folks who claim nymphing under an indicator to be "high art" just the same as the "dry-fly-only" crowd. It's all good.

Do it all. Do it all in the same day, knowing when, where, and how to react accordingly, and that's a great day! —**KD**

98. The Strip-Set

Much like the double haul, the strip-set is an acquired skill. It's also not just for saltwater fishing, but that's likely where it's used most often.

The strip-set is exactly what it sounds like. Rather than raising the rod and letting the supple rod tip "set" the hook, the strip-set involves you "stripping" the line in with your off hand when you feel a fish hit. This is vital for most saltwater fish, like permit and bonefish, but I've found it particularly effective in fresh water, too, particularly for predatory fish that hammer streamers, like pike, brown trout, and bull trout.

I also use the strip-set when chasing carp in shallow water, which can behave a lot like bonefish or redfish when they're feeding. A good strip-set secures the hook in the fish's jaws and lets you give a fish some line until you can get it on the reel. —**CH**

99. Micro-Drag. Where You Stand Makes a Huge Difference

I was fishing with guide Steve Greaney on a clear river in the Kahurangi National Park in the "top of the South" (northernmost part of the South Island of New Zealand). We were sneaking up on a bruiser brown trout (about 7 pounds, we guessed), and just

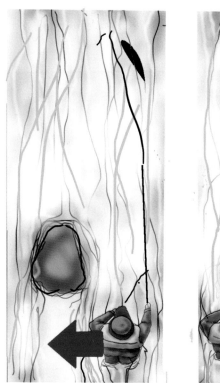
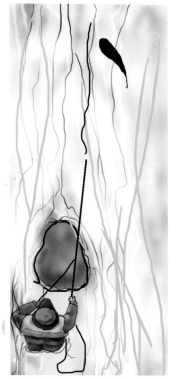

as I was about to unfurl my cast, Steve grabbed me by the shoulder and asked me to take two small steps to the left. You see, I was standing in shallow but briskly moving water. When I stepped left, I got behind a rock where the current was slack. The thing is, after I make a cast, I of course strip in the slack line as the fly and line drift back toward me (and the fly hopefully finds the feeding zone for the trout). But as I throw that line down toward my feet, if the current grabs it, it could create micro drag, even if I'm braking the line with the index finger on my casting hand. Finicky Kiwi trout pick up on even the slightest drag and will not only refuse, they'll slink off, meaning you have to hike probably another few hundred yards to find another fish. The subtle difference between standing in slack water instead of standing in moving water has really improved my hookup odds wherever I now fish. I now try to cast from slower water (or no water) whenever possible. For the record, we did catch that fish. It actually weighed 8 pounds. New Zealand fishing is all about details. The most important details typically happen after your fly hits the water. Watching where you stand is smart advice when you're planning two moves ahead. —**KD**

100. **Minimize Drag with Longer Leaders**

A nine-foot leader might be the standard leader for most trout anglers and, generally speaking, that's good enough for most situations. But in waters that have conflicting currents where the water you're casting from is moving slower than the water you're casting over, drag becomes a real problem—in fact, it might be the single biggest inhibitor to catching trout.

In addition to learning how to complete a really good upstream mend, try adding a few feet to your leader and consider using more supple leader material for the tippet. On bigger water, where I tend to encounter varying currents more often, I will add about five feet to my leader. Coupling the longer leader with a good upstream mend usually gives my fly more time to drift naturally through the strike zone before the drag eventually catches up to it and sweeps it downstream. It'll take some practice to cast that longer leader, but you'll find that you'll enjoy longer, more productive drifts once you get it down. —**CH**

101. **Casting at Taillights**

I got another great Kiwi guide tip from helicopter pilot and guide Dion Matheson. He said when sight casting at a fish in clear water, you don't want the fly (and leader and tippet) to

land directly upstream on a line with the fish. You certainly don't want the *fly line* to land above or upstream of the fish (lining the fish), regardless of its color. But even clear leaders and tippet can spook big, old, smart fish.

Dion said to imagine looking at the back of a car. The fish is centered, directly downstream of where the license plate is. Your best cast should be aimed toward one of the taillights—the one that's on the current (feeding lane) side of the fish. When the water is really clear, he or she is going to see that fly, trust me. If you make a good cast, and the line is behind the fish's conical range of vision, that fish will eat that fly if it wants to. If it doesn't, switch bugs. But by casting at the taillights, and not monkeying around with your tippet and fly drifting right over the fish's noggin, you give yourself the opportunity to switch, wait, and make another shot. We spent almost an hour doing just that with one fish, and I'll admit I was a little frustrated and thinking, "Jeez, maybe we should cast a little closer in line with the trout." But Dion urged me to stay the course, and sure enough, once we found the magic pattern, the fish eased over a few feet and sucked that fly down like nobody's business. —**KD**

102. **Covering Water**

On a recent trip to Patagonia, I earned the ire of my guide for the day, a diminutive Argentine named Santos, after I started casting to just about every rising fish I found.

"No," he told me flatly. "You must first cover the water in front of you."

He proceeded to tell me that, using the same length of fly line, I was to cast to the left, to the middle, and finally to the right, hitting structure, seams, and casting over depth the entire time.

"But what about that?" I asked, pointing to yet another hefty rise fifty feet upstream.

"When you work your way there, you can cast over it, too."

It seems a little . . . deliberate. Maybe too structured for some freewheeling anglers who like to kind of freelance their way up a trout stream. But, in all honesty, covering water with algebraic efficiency works, and in places like Argentina, where every inch of a beat is priceless (because once you reach the end of your beat, you're done), presenting a fly to every fish in the stream makes the most sense. —**CH**

103. **Moving Water and Moving Fish**

Let's face it, fly fishing for trout and fly fishing on the saltwater flats are really two entirely different sports, played with the same basic tools. In the salt, the cast is the price of admission. If you cannot make an accurate sixty-foot cast with a fly rod, within about four seconds, you need to go back to the fresh water pond and practice more. That said, despite what others might tell you, I'd say that in trout fishing, the cast is important, but not nearly as important as other things like your drift. Fly selection is about ten times more important in trout fishing than it is in the salt. You should fight saltwater fish completely differently with a fly rod than you would fight a trout (more on that in just a bit). But the biggest difference between the two brands of fly fishing is presentation.

It's actually pretty simple when you really think about it. In a river, the fish are nearly stationary, and the water is moving, bringing their food to them on a conveyor belt. And as an angler, your job is to sync up with that conveyor belt as much as you possibly can, making your flies look as natural and completely influenced by the whims of the currents as possible. A perfect drift is "spoon feeding" that bug right toward a feeding trout, in a way that looks as completely natural as possible.

In the salt, the water of course is still coursing and moving on factors like tides, albeit more subtly, and the fish tend to be cruising, looking for something to eat. So a saltwater fish, like a bonefish, tarpon, or permit, does not necessarily want to be "spoon-fed."

That lesson was ingrained in my angler mind many years ago when I was fishing with the late, legendary Florida flats guide Bill Curtis in Biscayne Bay. He was on the poling platform, and I on the casting deck, when a massive permit (it looked like a metallic trash can lid shining under the surface) came cruising into view. We both saw it right away, at the same time. I uncorked a beautiful cast (at least I thought so) about sixty feet, a few feet in front of the fish, and a tad just beyond. I gently started stripping a crab pattern back into what I thought would be the "zone," but that permit immediately turned and bolted off across the flat. Bill Curtis was already climbing down off the poling platform (which, incidentally, he invented) before I even started stripping the fly toward the fish. Dumbfounded, I had to ask, "What did I do wrong?" I thought I'd made a perfect cast.

Bill simply grumbled, "Permit aren't used to their food attacking them."

Point well taken.

If you want to catch fish in the salt, or in a river, you need to make your fly behave exactly like the natural food behaves. That means a baitfish or a crab in the salt is escaping. A little minnow in a river that tempts the brown trout on the bank is escaping. It has to show up in the field of vision, and then boogie. A nymph or a dry fly is totally at the mercy of the current. And that fly can't be waking around like a miniscule version of the "Miss Budweiser" hydroplane racing boat or the fish won't eat that either.

Tune in to what the fly you are throwing is supposed to represent—not only in terms of size and color and profile, but also in terms of action. When it's a scared little baitfish, it must act like a baitfish escaping for its life. And when it's a tasty little dun fly, drying its wings and getting ready to lift off, it needs to look totally oblivious and at the mercy of the water currents it's riding on.

Don't make salty presentations on the river, and don't make river presentations on the flats. Know the difference and play the game accordingly. —**KD**

104. **Skate and Twitch Big Flies in Low Light**

Nico, an Argentine fly-fishing guide based out of San Martín de los Andes, showed me a great trick that helped extend the fishing day on the famed Malleo River one spring. As the temperatures dropped once the sun disappeared behind the Andes, Nico tied a giant Fat Albert to the end of my tippet and instructed me to let it swing in the current. Once the line pulled tight, he instructed me to let it skate and to twitch the fly, making a few gurgles and splashes.

On my second swing, a nice brown hammered the twitching foam bug. It was the coolest take of a day full of cool takes.

The message? In low-light conditions, often, the trout are more tuned in to the sound and the motion of a fly. Also, the light likely just allowed the fish to see a silhouette, not the actual color of the fly. The skated and twitched bug likely looked like a big struggling terrestrial bug . . . or even a small mouse.

Next time the sun sets behind the mountains, give this trick a shot. —CH

105. Timing Is Everything on Dry-Fly Presentations

My friend Matthew Supinski, a decorated Michigan dry-fly guide/guru and the guy who literally wrote the book on brown trout and Atlantic salmon, reminds me that the absolute worst time to cast at a rising fish is right after it has eaten off the surface. It's made the effort, it's looking back down, it's deciding if that was worthwhile—it's not immediately going to whack away at another bug in a fraction of a second. But raise your hand if you've instinctively seen a fish rise and tried to laser a cast right on top of the trout as quickly as possible. My hand is raised.

In the trout world, everything is timed. If I know a hatch is happening, and the trout are keyed on certain bugs (as opposed to the opportunistic terrestrial take), I won't even make a cast until I've seen the same fish eat three times. I know what the

bug is. I know where the fish is. Now I need to know what the rhythm is . . . and I try to establish a timing pattern (does the fish typically eat every ten seconds . . . thirty seconds?) with which to sync that next cast. If you can close that timing loop, your dry-fly prowess improves incrementally. —**KD**

106. **Rod Tip Down for Streamers**

Fly fishing for trout or any predatory fish with streamers can be incredibly fun. But a lot of fly fishers, particularly those who spend a lot of time nymphing or casting dry flies, make one elementary mistake when chucking heavy flies and stripping them in.

When retrieving streamers on the swing or the strip, make sure your rod tip is down, and make sure you're keeping as tight a line as possible. This simply reduces the time between the hit and the set (and it's a strip-set, remember?).

On a trip to Argentina for trout, I even had a guide who recommended that my rod tip be just under the surface of the water. This, he explained, eliminated the "bounce" that often accompanies a strip. Oddly, I had a Bahamian flats guide recommend the same thing to me while fishing for bonefish—tip just under the water's surface—for the same reason.

It's good advice from the experts, and it will lead to more fish being hooked and caught. —CH

107. Looking Up

Baby salmon, as they are flushed downstream, typically face upstream. That helps them get oxygenated water through their gills. Caddis flies also often position themselves facing upstream as they land and lay eggs on the river.

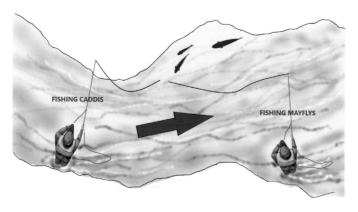

FISHING CADDIS

FISHING MAYFLYS

So what does that mean to you, the angler? It means that a downstream presentation during caddis fly hatches, or smolt bust streamer situations (like on the Naknek River in Alaska), is smart. Which direction your fly faces when it is near the fish could really matter.

You must be stealthy, of course, and be wary in all situations when you are presenting downstream. But with caddis hatches, and smolt busts and so forth, you want that fly facing upstream at the point of presentation. Downstream-up casts might make for a better drift, but in certain circumstances, upstream-down, minus the drag, is the only way to be really natural. —**KD**

108. Nymphs on the Swing

Nymphs aren't just for dead drifting, particularly in rivers with lots of tailouts and riffles. High-sticking traditional attractor nymphs like a Prince or a Copper John through a fishy run still makes sense, but what also makes sense is allowing the nymph to swing out on the tail end of a drift. This brings the fly closer to the surface, where trout often view it as an emerging bug.

Letting the nymph "swing out" even works under an indicator—it's not just for the Euro-nymphing crowd. —**CH**

109. Step When You Streamer

Learned this one from "Mad Max" Mamaev, a Russian guide who splits the months of every given year between Kau Taupen, guiding for sea-run browns in Tierra del Fuego, Argentina, and the Ponoi on the Kola Peninsula of Russia—arguably the most productive Atlantic salmon fishery in the world. Max is

probably the most innovative guide I have ever met. He even fashioned his first waders out of a chemical warfare military suit from the Cold War era.

So we were wading and casting at sea-run browns on the Rio Grande in Argentina. It was the "witching hour," meaning about 11 at night, as the sun was starting to fade. That's when the browns start to really get it on. But I would cast, and then take a tentative step downstream, and cast again. We were swinging big articulated black streamers off floating lines, using two-hand rods to cover the swath. Max said, "Step more . . . move!" and I thought he was full of beans, so I handed him the rod. Of course, two casts later, he was tied into a sixteen-pound sea-run brown trout.

The lesson learned, and the point is this: If you diddle your way along as you are swinging streamers, you only telegraph your presence to the fish. They don't want to see it coming five different ways. For a fish to attack a swung streamer, they want it to appear all of the sudden.

Move too fast, and you blow by fish. Move too slow, however, and you telegraph your presence.

I took this lesson home, and it works whether I'm swinging streamers on the Pere Marquette in Michigan or the Upper Colorado River. Stick and move with streamers. Make the cast and drift you love, then take three grand steps downstream before you fire again. This applies to steelhead or any other fish you are swinging for. Movement increases your odds, it doesn't hurt them. —**KD**

110. **Casting Streamers Upstream**

Streamers aren't just for swinging or stripping through currents. Streamers cast upstream and retrieved downstream, particularly for wading anglers, often elicit violent strikes from trout.

I've known this trick for a while, although it's not my first option when I tie a streamer to my tippet. But I watched recently as a tenkara angler employed the technique while fishing a deep, soft riffle in Patagonia (yes, streamers on a tenkara rod). He would flip the heavy fly upstream and then let it drift down, tugging every second or so on the rod to lift the fly off the bottom.

I was skeptical until I saw him land a twenty-one-inch brown. Twice.

I tried the method with a traditional fly rod and I, too, was rewarded with a fat brown. Don't discount streamers when you're fishing upstream. Often bait like crawfish, minnows, and sculpins will retreat downstream when they're threatened. It's not really a trick—it's an effective technique that imitates natural bait behavior. —**CH**

111. **Babysit Your Flies**

So much is made of the notion that once you drop your flies on the water, you don't want to mess with them, lest the trout see you tinkering about and refuse to eat. A trout won't eat it unless it looks just right, and natural. If you need to make a few tweaks to make that fly look natural, make them. For goodness sake, don't simply float a whacky, abnormal, obviously counterfeit fly over a feeding trout just because you were lucky enough to put it there in the first place.

I want my flies looking right, even if I have to tweak them, or babysit or whatever, whenever they are in the zone. A perfect natural pattern that looks absolutely false is far less effective than the kinda-close pattern that behaves like a real bug as it rides the water.

If you know (or think you know) where the fish really is, be dang sure that fly is riding right and looking like something a trout wants to naturally eat before it floats over its head. If it takes twitches and tweaks before you hit the bona fide feeding zone, fine, make them. Make all your tweaks right before you think that fly rides through the zone . . . and once you are there, don't move a muscle. Play the hand you've dealt yourself. Tweak before the zone. Don't futz around in the zone. —**KD**

112. **Top Water for Predators**

There's nothing more rewarding than the top-water take. From a six-inch brookie nailing a dry fly in a remote mountain stream to a barracuda slashing at a gurgler on a Bahamian flat, getting fish to eat on top is perhaps the ultimate rush in fly fishing.

But, for a lot of predators, top-water eating is a big part of what they do. Unlike trout, which get about 90 percent of their food from subsurface sources, many toothy predators often look up for food.

The idea is simple. Injured baitfish, frogs, struggling insects caught in the surface film, and swimming mice are all part of the diets of fish like northern pike and bass. In the salt, gurglers stripped across flats and around structure often bring big predators to the top, like redfish, barracuda, and even sharks.

Several years ago, while fishing the Tongass National Forest in southeast Alaska, a few of my fishing buddies and I were able to get migrating pink salmon to hit gurglers in the estuaries of the rivers off Admiralty Island.

The retrieves may vary. For mice and big trout, you might want a consistent pull to imitate a rodent just trying to get from one side of the river to the other. For bass and pike, you'll likely want something that moves water and looks like it's struggling. For saltwater fish, you may want to move a gurgler with real purpose. Regardless, top-water flies imitate real food for predators.

Having a good selection of poppers, gurglers, and mice in your fly box gives you the chance, when conditions are right, to enjoy one of the most dramatic moments in fly fishing. Don't chase predators without them. —CH

113. You'll Never Beat a Fish into Submission with Dry Flies or Streamers

Anglers from around the world are generally very respectful of their American counterparts—we're typically seen as generous sorts, and the wide-open spaces Americans enjoy as a birthright through our public lands and national and state parks are envied by many. But if we have one trait that confounds others around the world, it's that many of us think that we can impose our wills on those fish and get them to conform to our agenda, one way or another.

It is a universal truth that the secret to advanced fly fishing is crossing the frontier from wanting to impose your will on the fish, to being willing to understand the will of the fish and reacting to that in a resourceful way. That's it. That's the golden rule.

But many times we (myself included) find ourselves thinking, "Dang it, the fish didn't eat that one, but it will *have to* eat this one!" And we throw the same fly in the same spot five seconds later.

I once had a guy on the *Field & Stream* "Fly Talk" blog say that he thought he could "simulate a hatch" by throwing the same bug—absent a natural hatch—in the same area over and over, so the fish would be thinking a real hatch was happening and would therefore "switch on." What a bunch of baloney. But then again, in blog land, where people can comment without using their real names, baloney is the norm.

Trust me, you will never beat a trout or any other fish I know of into submission. If you make a good enough cast, and your fly is in the range where a fish sees it, and you know it, and the fish doesn't eat . . . there's only one smart next move. Switch patterns and wait. Right then. —**KD**

114. **You Can Beat a Trout into Submission with Nymph Patterns**

I've spent a lot of time in scuba gear in rivers watching trout. When it comes to trout eating nymphs, I can tell you that they will eat them in an opportunistic way. Imagine you're sitting on

the couch at a friend's house watching the football game, and there's a bowl of mixed nuts on the coffee table. You're going to nibble here and there—if you're like me you can't help yourself! That's how trout pick off nymphs. When they eat a grass-hopper off the surface, on the other hand, that level of com-mitment is like firing up the grill, seasoning the steak, cooking it (medium-rare), and topping it off with a little chimichurri. Indulgent protein reward, but not something you do all day every day.

The thing is, the trout munching on nymphs isn't typically moving six or eight feet to grab a bug, they are just dipping into that bowl of nuts in a zone where the bugs are consist-ently floating by. Moreover, trout don't only suck in bugs—I've seen them inhale twigs, leaves, and other bits of flotsam that drift by. Of course, they spit that stuff right out, just as they would your artificial fly once they realize it's a fake. A good hookset is all about reacting in that split second, and that's why even the best nymph anglers I know miss about half the half the strikes when a fish eats their nymph (at least that was my best guess as I watched it all unfold from the river bottom). If you hit 'em in the noggin, if you put your fly in that bowl of nuts on the coffee table, there's a decent chance that fish is going to pick it up sooner or later. It's all a matter of finding that zone, and yes, you can put that fly in the zone over and over, and so long as you don't spook the fish, you might eventually get bit. Depth and speed are the key factors, and I think my friend Pat Dorsey offers the best nymph fishing lesson of all when he says, "The difference between a good nymph angler and a great one is often a BB."

One of the most effective nymph patterns ever created in my opinion is John Barr's "Copper John." (Its worldwide popularity evidenced by the time I pulled a red #16 Copper John out of my flybox on a remote river in Chile, and the local guide with whom I was fishing smiled and said with enthusiastic approval, "Ah, sí. . . El Cobre de Juan!") Why is it an effective nymph pattern? It isn't because it looks super "buggy"; rather, it is a supremely efficient self-sinking fishing weight that happens to look just enough like a bug to get eaten.

In my opinion, the nymph game is more a matter of mastering physics, while dry-fly fishing is tilted more toward biology, and streamer fishing is probably somewhere in between. A guide with newbie clients is smart to fish a nymph rig if the goal is ultimately to feel a tug and land some fish, precisely because you *can* beat a trout into submission with a weighted nymph rig and a strike indicator.

My author friend John Gierach probably summed up the evolution of nymph fishing with more concise insight (as Gierach is prone to do) when he wrote: "It was our generation that took nymphing from something a respectable fly fisherman just didn't do, to something a respectable fly fisherman didn't do in front of witnesses, to a minor tactic that was good for a few extra trout between rises, to a method so effective that some saw no reason to fish any other way." —**KD**

115. **High School Memories**

I think I got a "C" in basic high school physics, and an "A" in AP biology, which probably explains why I enjoy dry-fly fishing a bit more than I do fly fishing with nymphs. —**KD**

116. **Move Your Feet**

Often, we're tempted to try and reach fish with our best hero cast. Generally speaking, this is a mistake. If you can get closer to your target without spooking the fish, do it. All of us are better anglers if the cast we have to make is as short and as tight as possible. Move your feet when you can. Save the rocket launcher for when you really need it. —**CH**

117. **A Fish Doesn't See Like Humans Do**

It's a mistake to assume a fish will sense you the same way humans sense things. The best example is vision: A fish's eyes are on the sides of its head, not pointing forward. Therefore, directly in front of/upstream is actually more of a blind spot than when your cast lands just a little bit off to the side. And the only true blind spot is directly behind—well behind—the fish. But they can sometimes still sense you if you're grinding your boots on gravel, splashing around, and so on. —**KD**

118. **Float Tubes and Garbage Cans**

I've never fully understood why we practice casting into a hula hoop flat on the ground, and then go stand thigh-deep in the water or sit in a float tube where the angles are all a few feet off. Two options for more accurate practice casts for people who wade deeper or fish from tubes a lot: 1) Practice casting while kneeling or 2) better yet, and far more comfortable, practice casting into the open top of a garbage can. —**KD**

119. **Profile Feeding vs. Color Feeding**

A great Kiwi guide like Nic Robertson will watch a fish work dry flies for several minutes before tying on a fly. If they notice the fish is feeding 70 percent to the left, and 30 percent to the right,

for example, they'll then take note of the position of the sun. If the sun is to one side of the fish, the fish will likely be "profile" feeding into the glare, albeit with less frequency (the 30 percent). On the side where the sun lights the flies better, the fish is "color" feeding (70 percent). Interestingly, you don't necessarily choose your fly and where you want to cast based on the feeding frequency percentages alone. You still want to plan that cast where you think you can make your best presentation. And yes, of course, you want to optimize your fly choices based on profile and colors, all the time. But if your best shot is in that "profile" lane, you might pick a bug that's a little more black and white, maybe with rubber legs. You want a "shadow dancer" on that side. If your best cast is on the color side, well, you might not settle for the generic parachute Adams; you might be a little more concerned with natural green or yellow hues. And you might even bump that cast just a few inches wider, just to instigate a charge. You don't necessarily want to drop that bug right on the beam and have the fish scrutinize it, lick it, think about it, or any of that. Seriously, think about the side and the sun when you dig into the fly box to pick the bug for your first best shot. —**KD**

120. **7X Is Overkill . . . Sometimes Literally**

Regarding fish handling, the scientists also tell me that the amount of time you spend fighting a fish has as much to do with its survivability as does keeping them wet. The longer the fight, the more you exhaust the fish, the more lactic acid builds, and so on. That's why I've never been a fan of "line class" world records and all that. I don't think I've fished 7X or lighter tippet in at least ten years, and I don't plan on changing that. I don't think there's anything that 7X tippet can solve that a precise cast and paying careful attention to your drift can't take care of better. —**KD**

121. **3X Tippet Should Be Your Baseline**

Kirk is absolutely right. Super-light tippet might seem like the answer to hooking really finicky trout, but if your goal is to hook, land, and release a fish in a healthy state, light tippet (6X or 7X, for instance) often spells doom for the fish you're trying to so hard to catch and then release. The fight lasts too long, and the fish just gets too tired—you can't "put the hammer down" for fear of breaking the tippet, so you "play" the fish until it's exhausted.

Bruce Staples, a renowned eastern Idaho angler and author, once told a group of anglers at our local fly-fishing expo here in Idaho Falls that 3X tippet is his go-to tippet diameter. That was years ago, and I've been following his lead ever since. —**CH**

122. **Fast Strip for Saltwater Predators**

For the most part, fly fishers can't strip fast enough to outswim a saltwater predator fish, be it a barracuda, a shark, or any predator that has its eye on your fly. The nice thing about fly fishing in salt water is that, by and large, it's a visual pursuit. Because of this, though, we tend to try and keep flies in the "target zone" when big predators start to pursue our offerings, and that's just not what prey fish do. Instead, strip faster. If there's anything a saltwater predator fish hates, it's letting a meal get away. As the

guides at the Palometa Club on the Yucatán's Ascension Bay explained to me as I slowed my retrieve to allow a fifteen-pound jack to get closer to the fly, "You can't strip it fast enough."

They're right. A baitfish in panic mode isn't going to slow down to be eaten. Strip faster. You'll be surprised how quickly the predator engages and eats. —CH

123. The "Jungle Angler"

I don't want to go too far off-script here, but I think it's worth saying that the fly-fishing realm involves a heck of a lot more than trout fishing, or steelhead and salmon fishing, or flats fishing for bonefish, permit, and tarpon. "Jungle angling" is the

real new frontier, and what's going on in South America in terms of exploring and stretching boundaries, is still, in a fly-fishing context, what the "golden age of safari" was for hunters in Africa one hundred or more years ago. If you want to taste the real, raw essence of nature on this planet . . . well, as an angler, there is no more honest place to do so than in the jungles of South America.

And there are lodges and such to help you experience the golden dorado (the gilded king of all fish), pacu, yatorana, ara-paima, and more species to mention right here—species that most American anglers have no idea exist in the first place. My experiences in the jungle have been mostly of the "exploratory" nature. It's hot, gritty, and unforgiving, but beyond imagination in terms of sheer natural beauty. There is no "cool side of the pillow" when you camp and sleep in the jungle. But when you come home, and you lay your head on your own pillow, you will hear the monkeys howl, and bugs hum, and birds call, for decades. I still hear the jungle, all the time.

Reaching certain points in the South American jungle can be easier (at least shorter) for the East Coast angler than reaching Alaska, and certainly New Zealand, or Chile or Argentina (farther south) can be. And you can learn many lessons in the jungle that apply quite favorably to fishing for trout and other species near home in North America.

Most important, you gain an appreciation for just how primal and unforgiving wild and native fish can be. It can be awe-inspiring, even frightening. For example, I once watched a fifteen-pound *temensis* peacock bass barrel toward a streamer fly I was stripping on the Rio Marie' in Brazil with gusto. But I lost my grip on the line, and *just that quickly*, the bass veered to the side with such momentum that it pounded headlong into a boulder. The predator instinct switched to fear instinct in a microsecond.

The fish was dazed and stunned, listing to its side. It only took about twenty seconds, however, for the local school of piranhas to show up and start nibbling at its tail and pectoral fins. Shocked back to consciousness, the bass wheeled and whacked the piranhas so hard that some flew out of the water in an explosive spray. And with that, the show was over, and all the fish scattered to the dark depths. It left a far more indelible impression than had I actually hooked and landed the bass in the first place.

My jungle experiences have led me to use streamers with barbell eyes far more often, even in trout rivers, if only to try to trigger that "predator" instinct a bit more.

It seems that every fish everywhere has a predator-prey/charge-retreat instinct, and that is influenced by a number of factors that dictate where they sit on the food chain, like the size of the fish (an eight-hundred-pound mako shark isn't afraid of much). And yes, human pressure seems to play into that also (it's a big commitment for a tailwater trout to decide to eat a dry fly rather than the little midges that are floating through its run in abundance, so that dry fly had better look like a T-bone steak).

One thing for sure, when you stop the strip on a lit-up fish charging a streamer, you almost always flip the "off switch" no matter where you are fishing, and no matter the species. —**KD**

124. **The Approach**

When you're wading the flats, the less noise you make—the less water you disturb—the better. I've had guides shake their heads in disgust at my "approach" to wading, and I've taken

their admonitions to heart. A good rule for wading bonefish flats: If you can hear water moving around your feet and legs when you're wading, you're making too much noise. The same is obviously true for permit.

But what about when the bottom is muddy, or if you're in waist-deep water? Antonio, a guide out of the Palometa Club in the Yucatán, taught me a very valuable lesson about deeper-water angling.

"Don't walk," he said to me as we walked across the soft bottom of the bay one afternoon, trying to get into casting position as a small school of permit worked its way toward us. "Skate."

Salt water is buoyant, even for a big guy like me. And Antonio was right. Get your feet out of the muck and use that buoyancy to your benefit.

And yes. We pulled a permit out of that school—my first ever. —**CH**

125. **Get Out of the Water**

When you're wading flats, sometimes actually getting in the water is a mistake. On tropical flats, where low-lying islands tend to pock the waterscape, sometimes it's best to step out of the water to cover more territory and make less noise. Also, even just a couple of feet of elevation can help you see your quarry better.

On the flats of Long Island, in the Bahamas, it's often easy to find little sand spits and worn-shell islands. I found that, often, I could spot incoming bonefish from the land and sometimes, I didn't even have to step foot in the water to make a good cast and eventually hook up. If you have the luxury of a bit of land, use it. —**CH**

126. A Kayak Is Your Ticket to Flats Mobility

I love to walk and wade for saltwater fish. One of my favorite places to do that is in the Lower Laguna Madre between the Texas mainland and South Padre Island. I've traversed miles of sand dunes on foot just to point my nose in the breeze and sight-fish to everything from sheepshead, redish, black drum, and even hardhead catfish.

But I learned quickly that mobility matters on the flats, and being able to move around a bit is key. That's where a kayak comes in. No, a kayak doesn't offer the convenience of

a full-on flats boat, but for a traveling angler, a kayak can be rented at a reasonable rate and it does give you the freedom to move around and alter your surroundings just a bit.

If you haven't tried a kayak, you'll be surprised at how easy they are to maneuver and how steady they are in the water, even for big people like me. A couple of years ago on a visit to the Yucatán, a fishing buddy and I rented a pair of kayaks and spent a day exploring a backwater lagoon that we would never have been able to reach had we not had the mobility. And, on the flats, kayaks help you keep a low profile, don't make much noise, and give you the flexibility to approach working fish without having to disturb the water by wading.

Today's kayaks are more convenient to fly fishers (they've always been easier for spin-casting anglers) than ever, as some models come equipped with elevated chairs, fly-rod-specific holders, and room for essentials, like a cooler for a few beers and compartments for fly-fishing gear.

If you haven't tried it, and you're interested, I think you'll find that it gives you a bit more freedom without the expense that comes with hiring out a guide and boat for a day on the water. It's a much more intimate experience and gives you an opportunity to really do some exploring and discovering on your own. —CH

127. Long and Fast for Pike

Northern pike are top-of-the-food-chain predators in lakes, rivers, and sloughs where they swim. They are instinctive creatures and when conditions are right, they can be caught at a regular clip on the fly. But sometimes, during unsettled weather or changes in water temperature, pike can seem almost completely uninterested in food. That's when you, as the angler, need to think like a pike and trigger that impulsive predatory strike.

I've fished with dozens of great Cree and Chippewa guides who grew up chasing pike in the boreal lakes of the North, and during slowdowns in the fishing, nearly all of them recommended to me that I speed up my strip, strip longer, and then bring the fly to a sudden stop. Pull. Stop. Pull. Stop. For most pike flies tied long, with marabou or rabbit strips, this retrieve causes the tail of the fly to kind of "catch up" to the head. It's a pulsation, and it gives off signals to any predator that mimics a baitfish in distress. As one Cree guide explained to me on a pike trip a few years back, "Everybody wants to change flies when the fishing slows down. That's a mistake. First, change the action of the fly." —**CH**

128. **Kneel Before the Trout**

My buddy Chad Shmukler and I had traveled clear across the hemisphere and were standing on a rocky bluff overlooking Argentina's Rio Malleo. It's a beautiful river; if you're familiar with the Arkansas River in Colorado, that's how the Malleo feels to me. It has similar topography, is about the same size, and has that same emerald hue to its deep, fishy pools.

As we stood atop the bluff looking down on the river, we were anxious. A pod of big rainbows was busy working an eddy during a prolific caddis hatch, and were game planning with our guide, Nico. While the Malleo isn't known for terribly spooky fish, we all knew that if we just wandered down the scree slope and started casting, we'd likely put the fish down.

The advice from the guide? Slowly creep down the slope and crawl to the riverbank. Then, Nico said, "Make your cast from your knees."

This reminded me of a much more intimate fly-fishing experience, this one in Shenandoah National Park in Virginia, where the quarry wasn't eighteen-inch rainbows, but eight-inch brookies in the smallish Hughes River. I'd managed to hook a few gorgeous brook trout, but I wasn't having the success I hoped. After slowing down and thinking about what I was doing, I figured out that I presented just too much of a silhouette to the fish. I began to creep up on the Hughes' deep plunge pools and started to cast from my knees to make myself a bit smaller.

Just as in Patagonia, I caught more fish. When you want to keep fish interested in a hatch, be more subtle. Start by kneeling before the trout. —**CH**

129. **The Kickapoo Weed Slide**

Fishing with my good friend Jon Christiansen in the Driftless Area of Wisconsin, we chanced upon a beautiful farm creek with undercut grassy banks where surprisingly large brown trout liked to hang out. We were fishing foam hoppers on a summer morning, and I made the mistake of hanging up my fly in the grass right above where I'd seen a big snout poke above the water surface only moments before. I gave a gentle tug to the line, and the fly plopped down on the water, and bang! Not long after, the same thing happened to—or rather for—Jon. Aggressive cast sticks fly in the grass . . . pull on the line . . . grasshopper falls into the water (*in much the same way a natural grasshopper would fall out of the grass and into the water*) . . . trout eats fly. After benefiting from poor casts richly rewarded a few times, we actually started trying to stick the flies in the grass, and sliding them off into the water, rather than splashing them straight on target with our casts, and it worked better that way. Granted, you have to have the right type of grass or weeds on the banks to pull this off. A bush that grabs a fly like Velcro won't work. But I've taken that idea to other places, especially when I'm fishing hoppers to the bank from a driftboat, and bouncing a foam bug off the rocks or sticking one in the grass and letting it slide into the water seems to be about as dirty a trick as you can pull on a trout lurking under the cut bank. —**KD**

130. **Ringing the Dinner Bell**

There's a total opposite scenario from when fish flee the loud plopping noise of a fly landing. Sometimes, they come running when they hear (or probably more appropriately, feel) something landing on the water. My buddy Al Keller used to take a pocketful of pebbles or seashells on his skiff, and when the tide was up and the snook were up under the mangrove roots where you couldn't really get a cast to them, he'd plop a shell or pebble out on the sandbar next to the mangrove. Sometimes the fish would poke their heads out, and we'd get a shot at them that way. Bass will do that too sometimes. I think it mostly depends on the fish . . . I've only seen trout behave like that in faraway places like Russia and Chile, where they haven't interacted with people much, if at all. —**KD**

PART FIVE

Miscellaneous

131. Tom's Leader

Tom Rosenbauer is probably the preeminent educator in the fly-fishing world today. During his more than forty-three years with the Orvis Company, Tom has written more books and articles than we can list; he now hosts a widely listened-to podcast, appears on television shows, and all that. Many anglers like myself, who have been around the block a few times, are only half-joking when we credit Tom with teaching us to fish, at least in part. Tom also happens to be a good friend. I've had the pleasure of fishing with him in places like the wilds of Chile, in the Colorado high country, in Montana, on the tradition-laden rivers in the Catskills, the flats in the Bahamas, and elsewhere. Tom is the real McCoy, not an "all hat, no cattle" author. Quite the opposite—if anything, he understates his own prowess in his writing. I still learn from him, and not long ago we were kicking back in the Hill Country of Texas, where I asked him for a few tips I could unceremoniously steal for this book. This was the best one:

Tom will borrow your fly rod. He'll use someone else's reel. He'll even borrow boots and waders in a pinch. But there's one thing of his own that Tom insists on using, every time, no exceptions. . .

His leader.

Now you might think that $5-$10 of monofilament and/or fluorocarbon attached to hundreds of dollars or more of gear might be a little lower on his priority list. But Rosenbauer says it's the number one thing he worries about—not only because that's the "connection" to the fly and fish, but also because a properly built leader (he builds or at least modifies his own) will do more to help the cast and presentation than most anglers are willing to acknowledge.

His recipe is simple: He extends the butt section by a few feet, matching the thickness of the end of the leader, and he extends the tippet by a few feet. This naturally makes for a longer leader, but that extension of the butt end helps you point and lay it down. The extra tippet, with the more supple material, is meant to help prevent microdrag.

Whether you build your leader exactly as Tom does or not doesn't matter. The lesson is that you should tinker with leaders and find something that works really well for you. Don't just take them out of the package, tie them on, and expect everything to be perfect. "Stock" leaders are no cure-all, and that comes from a guy who's been working for a company that sells packaged leaders. —**KD**

132. **Carp: Not Just for City Kids**

Carp were among the first fish I caught as a kid growing up in the suburbs of Denver. I lived a short bike ride away from a

city park that had a couple of muddy ponds surrounded by manicured grass and the usual sharp-edged jungle gyms and take-your-life-into-your-own-hands playground equipment. I remember mixing up dough balls in little plastic sandwich bags and riding my bike down to the park to go fishing. And when the fishing was slow, I'd risk my existence on the rusty old jungle gym.

I caught a lot of carp. As a kid, these rangy omnivores were the perfect "gateway drugs" into more "advanced" fishing. As I matured as an angler, I left the carp behind and began to focus on trout and other more "acceptable" gamefish.

Then, about twenty years ago, while fishing for smallmouth bass on southern Idaho's Snake River, I rediscovered carp as the gamefish astute fly fishers are now targeting again. Carp might be the most cherished gamefish the world over, and it's easy to see why. They're smart and strategic. They have a varied diet and can be incredibly picky. And they fight. Hard.

And, of course, they're found just about everywhere.

Fly fishing for carp is among the most challenging aspects of the craft, as flies must be presented perfectly. Anglers must be stealthy and astute. And then there's the battle. Hands down, carp are the strongest, hardest- and longest-fighting fish I've encountered in fresh water.

I've come full circle in my fishing journey. From dunking a ball of flour, salt, and water into the depths of a city drainage pond to sight-casting to cruising carp in the shallows of the Snake, I am not ashamed to say that carp are more than likely the fish of my lifetime. Think about it. I bet I'm not the only angler out there who feels that way. —**CH**

133. **What I Really Have to Say About Carp**

They stink. They're ugly. They're slimy. They're absolutely gross fish. But no fish, in fresh or salt water, will bring out the "next level" in a fly angler like the common carp can.

I almost cannot comprehend the fact that they were introduced in this country around the same time that brown trout were brought to American rivers—and the carp were the prized fish, guarded under arms as a food source, while the browns were considered merely play things. Fast-forward a century or more, and there's a "Trout Unlimited" because trout are fragile fish, the piscine "canary in the coal mine" whose higher purpose, to be completely honest, is to telltale the health of cold, clean water in America. Carp . . . jeez . . . they've proven to be the supreme adaptors. We can't kill those things if we try, and we try. And yes, they are nuisance species in many places. They out-compete other species (like trout) and often ruin a good thing. I hate carp sometimes.

But the angler in me adores and respects carp. Because they can sense you—smell you, feel you, hear you—like no other fish on the planet. And in certain situations, they are the absolute toughest fish to master with a fly rod. They eat off the surface, but they don't. They grub for crayfish . . . when they feel like it. You spook one, and it tells all the other fish around it. Boot one fish, and you boot them all.

I have many friends who chase carp as a primary passion. For the most part, they are kind, fun-loving, interesting, and wonderful people. But they're also pretty damn twisted and weird. They're going to love the fact that I just wrote that, because they also have well-earned confidence. Put it this way: The really good fly-fishing-for-carp anglers consider species like steelhead trout and permit "easy" fish. And I am not just stating that for effect, because I can tell you that I've watched carp gurus absolutely own many bonefish flats and trout runs.

Here's the bottom line. Hold your nose and go try to catch carp on a fly. It's not a fad, and it's not a marketing trick that revolves around the (very true) fact that carp are everywhere, and accessible to any fly angler anywhere in the United States. As you read this, for 90 percent of you, the closest fish that will eat a fly if you know how to show it to them, right now, is a carp. And they'll demand A-game angling by way of casting, presentation, fly selection, and so forth, like no other fish can. If you want to elevate your fly-fishing game to an elite level, you must at least dabble with carp now and then. —**KD**

134. Urban Angling

Sometimes, the best fishing is found close to home. Thanks to water quality improvement (thank you, Clean Water Act) across the United States over the last fifty years or so, some urban fisheries can compete nicely with more far-flung angling destinations. Certainly, you'll have to adjust your expectations, and likely understand that, alongside the prized trout and bass that we might love to pursue, you might also find yourself casting to rangy carp and bullhead.

Some of my friends who live in Washington, D.C., swear by the fishing in the Potomac River as it runs right through the city. What used to be a river people avoided for fear of getting sick is now a thriving urban fishery for everything from

striped bass and shad to bass, panfish, catfish, and introduced northern snakeheads from Asia. A couple of my more serious angling friends are even targeting long-nose gar in the river and its tributaries.

In urban downtown Denver, astute city anglers are targeting trophy trout in the South Platte. Growing up as a kid, the Platte was considered a conduit for sewage and not many folks ever considered its potential as a fishery. Things are different today.

We can thank half a century of water-quality protection for the revival of many urban waterways.

But, just as in more pristine fishing destinations, the same rules apply. Structure matters. A submerged rock in a pristine mountain stream might be replaced by a grocery cart or a car muffler that tumbled into the river several years back after an urban drag race. That "structure" still provides fish with what they need to survive and thrive: protection and opportunity.

If there's a river or stream running through your community, chances are there are fish in it. And where there are fish, there is angling opportunity, and often that opportunity is close to home. Don't just write off the city ditch as a polluted, unfishable eyesore. Next time you wander by it, stop and look for fish. You might be surprised. —CH

135. Snip Your Tippet at a 45-Degree Angle

That way you create a "pointy" end to stick through the eye of your hook. It's hard enough trying to thread tippet through the eye of a small fly, especially if you need glasses to see things clearly in close. It's harder when it is a blunt end, whether you're using 3X or 6X. But if you turn your hand ever so slightly as you clip your tippet, and cut on about a 45-degree angle, that pointed end of the tippet will find the eye of the hook sometimes when you cannot. Try it, and you'll be surprised how much faster you can thread the eye with a pointy tippet. This is one of those subtle pro guide moves that improves efficiency, especially for those with challenged eyes. Can't ever hurt the cause either! This one is from Daniel Hackett, guide/owner of Riverfly1864 in Launceston, Tasmania. —**KD**

136. **Weight an Unweighted Fly with Fly-Tying Beads Instead of Split Shot**

We can tie flies with weight, using wire or beads, or we can add weight to our rig using split shot (lead-free, please!).

But have you thought about using traditional fly-tying beads while fishing to add weight to a streamer of a nymph rig? Here's why I like it: it allows you to quickly change the weight for something lighter or heavier and, when fishing, it looks more like something that's part of the fly, rather than just a hunk of tungsten pushing magically through the water ahead of your fly pattern.

Fly-tying beads come in many sizes and many weights. Having a few on hand while you're on the water makes good sense, and it gives you the flexibility to change the depth of your fly simply by tying a loop knot like a perfection loop. I just slide my bead of choice, small hole first, loosely onto my tippet, and then I tie my fly on using the perfection loop (see illustration for the setup). When the streamer is pulled through the water, the bead rests just above the hook eye and the knot in the perfection loop—it's not pinched onto the tippet, and it slides freely.

I got this tip from watching Colin McKeown of *The New Fly Fisher* as he was trying to find the right depth for landlocked Atlantic salmon in Labrador. I've since come to believe that this might be the best way to add weight to streamer patterns while you're on the water. I've also used smaller beads to add weight to nymphs, with good success.

Not only does the bead add weight to your pattern, but you can fish different colors, different sizes, even different types of beads, ranging from small brass beads to large conehead beads. It just adds some flexibility to your angling. —**CH**

137. The Perfection Loop for Tying on Flies

This easy knot is used by many peacock bass guides in South America. If you trust the perfection loop for connecting a leader to a fly line, you can also trust this one to hold a fly reliably.

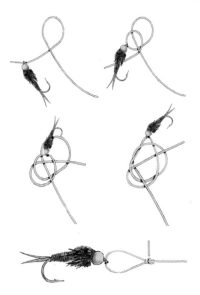

138. Four Easy Hacks to Save Money

With all apologies to my fly-shop friends: 1) Hard-as-Nails nail polish is a pretty darn reliable head cement for tying flies; 2) The fingernail clippers I can buy at the drugstore or grocery (like the ones my grandfather had clipped to his vest his whole life) do about as good a job of cutting leaders and tippet materials as any pair of $50 nippers will; 3) A mixture of hand lotion and lighter fluid makes for decent dry-fly flotant; and 4) a ziplock bag of uncooked rice will wick water out of a large dry fly about as well as the high-dollar tiny bottle of magic powders we buy all the time. —**KD**

139. **The Twenty-Minute Rule**

When I'm fishing for trout in high-elevation streams, I try to adhere to a simple rule that generally puts me on more fish and in places where fewer anglers are likely to go. If there's a trail along the creek (and most streams in high-country locales, wilderness areas, and the like are paralleled by trails), I make a point to walk at least twenty minutes away from the trailhead before I start fishing.

Yes, you often walk past some good water within that twenty minutes, but I find that most casual anglers won't put in the footwork needed to get away from water where trout see a lot of flies. I've been known to walk for a good hour or more before I'll stop and fish, but my fishing algebra has deduced

that twenty minutes is a good minimum, and for fleet-footed hikers, that can be a mile or more away from the trailhead.

I fish a lot in Yellowstone National Park. Every year, about 150,000 anglers buy park fishing licenses, which means storied rivers like the Firehole, the Madison, and the Yellowstone are going to see plenty of anglers, and the fish that swim there are going to see plenty of flies. But the smaller creeks and back-country lakes and streams don't get too much pressure, even with all that "competition" in the park. Just by walking twenty minutes away from where everybody else starts fishing, you can put yourself in relative solitude and cast over trout that don't see flies every day. —CH

140. The Ten-Second Rule

Much has been written and said about fish handling, keeping fish wet after you catch them, and all that. I'm all for keeping fish in the water. But if you play around with a fish in the net

(and in the water) for ten minutes, you're probably going to do more harm to it than you would by lifting it out of the water for a few seconds, snapping a quick photo, and letting it go. The latest advice from the science team at Trout Unlimited is to follow a ten-second rule. Minimal handling, then ten seconds of airtime, max, then let the fish go. Not ten seconds, put them back in the water, then take another photo for a few more seconds, then "give them another drink" and let them go. Ten seconds max. Count bananas, Mississippi's, whatever works for you, out loud or in your head, but before you hit eleven, that fish should be back in the water and released. This fish was out and back in in about four seconds. And it was fine. —**KD**

141. **Get in Shape. Stay in Shape.**

My friend Craig Mathews used to own and operate Blue-Ribbon Flies in West Yellowstone, Monana, along with John Juracek. Between the two of these fly-fishing icons, more knowledge about the fish and the fishing of the Greater Yellowstone Ecosystem has likely been forgotten than most will ever acquire.

If John is a casting guru (and he most certainly is), Craig is a fly-fishing sensei. One recent autumn, while dropping in on a series of fly-fishing seminars in Island Park, Idaho (about thirty minutes from West Yellowstone), I heard Craig offer the seminar students some really great advice (and, of course, it's easier said than done).

"Get in (or stay in) excellent physical condition."

Seems simple, right? I mean, all of us want to continue fly fishing for years to come. But how many of us are willing to put down the cheeseburger and pick up the salad fork? How many of us, as we get older, can make time for the gym instead of opting for a beer or a cocktail at the local pub?

I'm the first to admit that the kind of fishing I like to do—walk-and-wade creek fishing and stalking tailing fish on flats—likely requires a bigger commitment than I've given it in recent years. Nagging ailments that started as rolled ankles on the high-school basketball court or back issues developed over years of fishing and hiking in remote waters have taken their toll, and my gym time needs to improve if I'm going to continue the kind of fly fishing I enjoy.

While being in excellent physical condition (something Craig has accomplished) may not be absolutely vital, being in good enough shape to wander along a mountain stream or wade a Bahamian flat certainly makes the act of fishing easier and more enjoyable.

Ultimately, the decision is up to us. I have a gym membership. Upon hearing Craig's advice, I'm going to start using it more. —**CH**

142. **High Rod and Low Rod**

I still feel bad for Al Keller. I apologize to him every time we fish together, and we still do that every few years. He's one of my favorite guides and best buddies in the whole fishing world.

It was many years ago when we were both just starting out—me as a budding outdoor writer, Al as a still wet-behind-the-ears tarpon guide in the 10,000 Islands in southwest Florida. My father-in-law hired Al to take us on a half-day charter, but my wife subbed in for her dad at the last minute.

I'll remember this forever. We were booking across a bay, and Al suddenly cut the boat motor and leapt up on the poling platform. I still have no idea how he did it, but he saw two laid-up tarpon from hundreds of yards away, and by the time the skiff's momentum had stopped we were slowly, silently sneaking right up on the fish from about one hundred yards out, and the tarpon hadn't moved a dime.

I got up on the front deck and stripped out some line. The boat slid within seventy feet. "Go ahead, take a shot," Al said. Looking at the closest big gray torpedo silhouette, I muttered back, "Which end is which?"

"Left side," he whispered. And so I let fly with a crisp and honest cast that plopped my fly about three feet from the tarpon. The cast turned out to be the only thing I did really well.

I still remember . . . I still dream about it decades later . . . watching that ancient dinosaur fish take notice, spin around, and then accelerate its tail motions. Then that big ol' bucket mouth inhaled that fly. I strip-set with three hard jerks (maybe the second thing I did right), and it was on! That tarpon bolted away and made a thunderous gill-rattling jump that made my knees knock. I bowed to that silver king, just as I'd been told (okay, maybe a third thing I did right), and when the tarpon crashed lengthwise on the flat, the noise shattered the calm, like a piano had been dropped from the sky.

We fought that fish for more than half an hour. But the whole time, I held my rod tip high to the sky. I was a trout fisherman, after all, and had ingrained in my mind to "keep that tip up!" with every fish I'd ever caught. Al, to his credit, was incredibly patient, and he urged me to lower the rod tip and fight the fish through the *line*, and not the rod. But I flailed, and eventually failed, when that fish found a deep bucket in the mangroves, and broke me off. Jeez . . . after all that!

When we got back to the boat ramp, Al kindly took me aside and had me hold the rod as he held on to the leader. He said, "Go ahead, pull me around with the rod tip high." And I pulled and flexed that rod until I thought it might break, but I didn't budge Al. And then Al said, "Now drop the rod tip, and pull on me with the line." Which I did, and I almost immediately tipped Al, still holding the leader, right over on his knees.

Lesson learned. That "tip-up" thing is good for smaller fish. It's good for steering around obstacles like tree stumps in a river, or coral heads when you have a bonefish on. But it isn't worth jack when you have a big boy on and you need to move that fish around to effectively fight it and land it.

And that's true for big trout, steelhead, salmon, and many other fish. Go ahead and pull on your fishing buddy if you don't believe me. You'll find that you can move something with a low rod position, even with 4X or 5X tippet. All that high rod tip does is ensure you a stalemate. If you want to dictate the fight, you must learn to fight fish through the line and leader, not just the rod. If I were to suggest a cutoff . . . I'd say two pounds. Anything over two pounds—for damn sure a one-hundred-pound tarpon—you need to be fighting that fish low and steering like reins on a horse's bit, not high like a maypole.

I'm sorry about that, Al. Still am. —**KD**

143. The Clouds Will Tell You

How tough will the day be? Rule of thumb: low deck steady cover, get ready for some dry-fly fishing; high and bright, almost no clouds at all, fish terrestrials too gaudy to refuse, or go deep.

That mixed layer of cloud cover, with some passing low, and an umbrella up high—well, that's the mixed bag because the conditions aren't stable. Those are usually the toughest fishing days when you absolutely need to keep your eyes peeled and react with speed. Those are the days when things literally change minute by minute. —**KD**

144. **Step Out of Your Comfort Zone**

Too often, we find ourselves homing in on particular fish, and I suspect we do this for a variety of reasons. First, we tend to focus on fish that we can find at hand. If, like me, you live in a place where trout are plentiful, it makes sense to fish more for trout than it does for anything else. Second, it's only natural that we slide into comfort zones when we fish—it's important for a lot of us to get *really* good at catching the fish we have close to home.

Several years ago, I took a trip to southwest Florida to try and chase redfish in the marshes around Sanibel and Captiva islands. I had been largely an inland trout guy—I had been content to chase trout up and down the Rockies, with frequent visits to Alaska for salmon and char and the occasional trip to the Northwest to give steelhead a try. Saltwater fishing for me was still new and foreign, and I found that trying to solve the saltwater riddle was exciting.

I didn't catch too many fish at first—the casting was different, the fish were unusual, the environment was completely unfamiliar . . . and a little scary. Once, while kayaking out of Matlacha, Florida at sunrise, I had a manatee surface right by my elbow, and it startled me so badly that I almost tipped the little craft. But, on that same adventure, while targeting redfish (and hoping for a tarpon), I managed to hook and battle a sailfin catfish. I did manage to hook and land a redfish, but the "sailcat" was easily the most fun I had that day. Later in the trip, while looking for snook off the beach, I got into a school of ladyfish that kept me entertained for hours.

Since that trip to Florida, I've made a point to try and make time every year to go after something besides the trout that swim in my home waters. I've been to the Okefenokee Swamp of southern Georgia for bowfin, the boreal lakes of Manitoba for pike, the Mayan Riviera for permit and bonefish, and the Arctic for grayling and char.

Not everybody has the means or the desire to travel to fish, but getting out of your comfort zone will only make you a better all-round angler. Even if you don't want to hop on a plane, chances are you can find different fish close to home to pursue with a fly rod. Even here, in the trout "center of the universe"—where the Henry's Fork, Madison, and South Fork are short drives away for trophy trout—I have been able to find great bluegill and bass ponds, and chasing carp in the river has become a passion.

I'm a better fly fisher for it, too. —**CH**

145. **Head Up, Game Over**

When you are playing a trout to the net, it's all about angles. If the fish is pointed nose-down, bulldozing toward the bottom, it's not ready, and if you try to horse it in, that's when you are likely to break off. When its head breaks the surface, however, the fish loses its leverage, and is at your mercy. I'm not talking about a

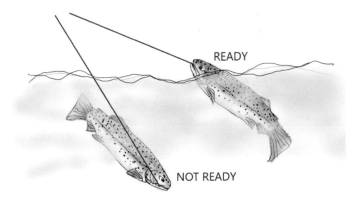

READY

NOT READY

jumping fish, of course. I'm talking about when the fish rolls at the surface, and you see its nose above the water. That's the exact point when to apply the pressure. If you are relentless, as you should be, you can almost skate them across the water and right into your net. Don't give them back their leverage. It's better for the fish if you land them and release them quickly. Once that head comes up, it should be game over. Give them the business. There are limits of course, but even a 20-incher on 5X tippet should be easy to land if you keep the rod bent, apply good pressure, and keep its head just a little bit above the waterline. This becomes a good habit after you practice long enough. —**KD**

146. **Dog on a Leash**
Speaking of that low rod tip and fighting fish: Even in a trout river, and even with an eighteen-inch trout, the endgame, as you pull the trout toward the landing net, is almost always better when

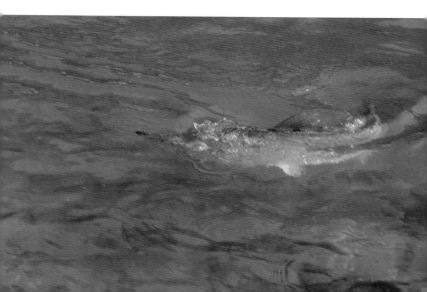

the rod tip is low. Sure, go ahead and fight 'em up high. But I watched the late, great Tom Whitley, who was an absolute master on the South Platte River in Colorado, make more anglers happy and create more big fish photos with his clients by teaching his sports to drop the rod tip near the water and steer the fish toward his landing net. I swear, it was almost like watching them walk a dog on a leash. Fight them up high, steer around the rocks, but once that fish is tired and in a flat water landing zone, you can drop the rod tip almost in the water, and pull them toward that net. It's almost like they're walking home. —**KD**

147. **Rod Weight Should Be Based on Fly Size**

A lot of people think the size of the rod they use should match the type of fish they're going after. Sure, that can play into it to some degree. But Jerry Siem, rod designer for Sage, once explained to me that the number one factor in choosing a rod should be the type of flies you are going to cast. Remember that the fly rod is meant to enhance your efficiency and make casting easier. Throwing big articulated streamers with a 3-weight isn't very efficient. On the other hand, casting Size 20 dry flies with an 8-weight doesn't make much sense either. The rod companies don't advertise this, but 75 percent or more of all fly rods sold in the United States are nine-foot 5 weights. Why? Because that weight is versatile enough to throw dry flies with feel, but it also has the oomph to toss a Woolly Bugger when you want to. If I know most of my fishing will be with mayfly or caddis dries on a given day, I usually fish a 4 weight. If I don't know what will happen, I'll take a 5 weight. Tossing large terrestrials in the wind, probably a 6 weight, and a dedicated streamer day is usually 7 weight for me. Everybody is different so don't consider that a rule, just a little advice. And you certainly don't have to have an array of fly rods that outnumber the irons in your golf bag . . . but it is fun. —**KD**

148. **Dry Your Fly First, Apply Flotant Second**

This may seem elementary, but I've watched many an angler—even some guides—pull a soggy fly from the water and try and blow it dry before plopping another dollop of flotant gel on the bug, thinking that's all it takes to resurrect a drowned fly. It's not.

The best way to bring a drowned fly back to life is with desiccant first—silica powder or "dry shake" that's made by a number of companies. Most "dry shake" bottles invite you to put the fly into a bottle containing the desiccant and shake it. This pushes the powder into the fly, pulling moisture from all of the pattern's feathers, hairs, and wraps.

Once it's really dry, blow the excess power from the bug and then apply more flotant if you choose. If you just put flotant on a fly that's soggy to the core, it just serves to lock that moisture in and sink your fly even faster over just a couple of casts. —**CH**

149. **Driftboat Rules**

There are two important rules for fishing with another angler out of a driftboat—one for the person up front, one for the tail gunner in the back. Person up front, you cast forward. If you

are casting behind the oarlocks of the boat at any time, it is perfectly okay for the person on the sticks, or the angler in the back, to rise up and throw you out of the boat. Person in the back, you are the eyes on the whole show, so time your casts accordingly. Any time there's a tangle, lines get crossed, casts get mixed up, or any of that, it's your fault, and you get to fix the mess.—**KD**

150. **Fly Reels for Trout Are Just Line Holders**

Trust me, I get it. It's *so* tempting to always have the latest and greatest when it comes to gear—it may be the single-most deceiving aspect of fly fishing: If you don't have the newest and the best, you're somehow phoning it in.

For fly rods, I suppose there could be some truth to that logic. For trout anglers, owning the latest fly reel with the disc drag and the large arbor and the best bar stock—well, don't fall victim to that notion.

First, unless you're regularly fishing to really big trout (like 20- to 22-inch fish), chances are, you haven't seen the backing on your fly reel since you put it on there. Second, most trout are brought "to the reel" using tight lines and series of strips, and this is usually done not to control trout, but to control fly line.

For trout anglers, the reality is that most fly reels are simply line holders. Owning the latest and greatest is nice, but it's certainly not necessary. If you're going to skimp and save money as a trout angler, consider a basic fly reel as a way to do it. An old click-and-pawl reel is likely all you need. —**CH**

151. **Fly Reels Matter Mostly for Saltwater Fish**

Unlike reels for trout angling, reels for fishing the salt are really important. Not only must they hold a lot of line (and a lot of backing), they must be durable and dependable. Saltwater fish, from tarpon and permit to bonefish and jacks, will push your gear to its limits.

Having good, well-crafted, and dependable fly reels that can resist the corrosion of the ocean and handle the long, fast runs of the strongest fish on earth is vital. Friction, drag, and quality construction really do matter.

The message? Don't skimp on saltwater reels. This is one of the aspects of fly fishing where the old adage "You get what you pay for" is absolutely spot-on.

And, while you're at it, take care of your gear when you're fishing the salt. A thorough freshwater rinse of your reel at the end of a day of fishing will help your reel last longer and stay in good condition. —**CH**

152. **Faster Rods Aren't Always Better**

Today's fly-rod manufacturers have become veritable wizards when it comes to crafting rods that can help anglers throw more line. "Fast" rods that are marketed as fly-line rocket launchers certainly have their place in the fly-fishing tapestry, but for a lot of anglers, fast rods are unnecessary.

Rods billed as "fast" usually "flex" more near the tip of the rod. This enables the rod to load better with more line stretched out of the tip, and that allows the rod to cast more line with the right casting motion.

"Slower" rods tend to flex closer to the middle of the rod, or even toward the grip. Fiberglass or bamboo rods are generally slower than graphite or composite rods (although that's not always the case), and tend to be slower. Also, slower rods tend to help anglers with more subtle presentations—the idea isn't always to throw eighty feet of fly line into the wind, but to more accurately place a modest cast on the water with very little disturbance.

What kind of rod do you need? Well, what do you fish for? Trout in spring creeks? You might consider a slower, more supple rod. Bonefish on the flats in a twenty-knot wind? That rocket-launcher 8 weight with the action of a broom handle might be more your speed. —**CH**

153. **Dirty Hats and the Spot-Free Rinse**

If you're like me, you have a hat or two that you really like, no matter how old. Maybe you think it's lucky. Maybe you just like how it fits. But because you like it so much, it gets dirty,

maybe smelly. But before you chuck it in the trash, try this. Stick it in your dishwasher, right there with your glasses, knives, forks, spoons, and plates. Run it through the cycle, take it out, let it air dry. See what happens. I'm wearing my favorite twenty-year-old hats that I find lucky, or which fit well, because they were rebirthed with a little Cascade among the after-dinner dishes. —**KD**

154. **You Get What You Pay for**

I've always been tempted by bargains, and occasionally, I can find one in the fly-fishing realm that puts a big smile on my face. But this is the exception to the rule. Generally speaking, when it comes to fly-fishing gear and equipment, you really do get what you pay for.

I've been reminded of this rule over and over again. Several years back, when Kirk and I were visiting Lake Athabasca and chasing big pike and lake trout on the fly, I arrived in Stony Rapids with a 7-weight fly rod I'd received in the mail a week earlier from a new manufacturer, to test while in the north. It looked like a nice implement—handsomely made, well-equipped with a fighting butt, and the general trappings that come with a heavier fly rod made for casting big flies to big fish.

And while the rod performed adequately, I was able to compare it to a truly fine fly rod that Kirk brought with him. The differences were noticeable. And, of course, so was the price point. Kirk's rod was fast and light. My 7-weight had a softer action and weighed noticeably more. I'm sure it was a fine rod, but when compared to a more superior product, it wasn't even close. I spent several days on the lake with fly-rod envy.

I get that the price point is important to a lot of fly fishers. Shelling out hundreds of dollars for rods, reels, waders, boots, packs, and the like isn't the part of fly fishing most of us enjoy. But, over the years, I've come to the conclusion that, most of the time, gear is priced based on its quality and its likely performance.

For instance, I went to Patagonia several years back, and I packed my gear in a double-compartment travel duffel that I found for a good price. It cost quite a bit less than the name-brand travel gear I could have gotten from the likes of Fishpond or Orvis, and I figured I might have found a real bargain. Long story short, the bag all but disintegrated on the flight to Buenos Aires, and I had to wrap it in plastic upon arrival just to keep all my gear from falling out. And then, when I got to San Martín, I had to pay top dollar for a new duffel, just to get through the trip. So much for the bargain.

I also tie most of my own flies. Over the years, I've transitioned from cheap tying equipment to really good tools that make my tying easier and make my flies more appealing and, just as important, more durable. The cheap stuff broke down sooner than I thought it should have. The more expensive stuff, if you take care of it, will last much longer and, in the long run, likely save you money.

The lesson? In the fly-fishing world, you really do pay more for quality. You can very occasionally find a bargain, but if you're serious about your fishing and you want your gear to last, save your money up and buy the good stuff. You'll be glad you did. —**CH**

155. The Timing on the Hookset Depends on How Deep the Fish Is

This can be frustrating! Fish one place, and see the trout rise to your fly; miss it and you're told "you're not quick enough." (I actually once had Tim Mosolf, the late legendary guide on Montana's Beaverhead, tell me, after I missed, but ended up foul-hooking a fish in its anal fin . . . "Oh that fish ate your fly, but it shit it out . . . you're *that* slow!") Fish somewhere else, and you seemingly rip the fly out of a trout's mouth because you reacted *too* quickly . . .

You can't win, right? What gives?

Daniel Hackett, my Tasmanian guide pal, says we need to consider the depth of the water that the fish is in when we factor how quickly to set the hook. If it slinks up from a depth of six feet or so to suck down that dry fly, set it when it's on its way back home, which means give a good pause. This is the situation when you might utter "God Save the Queen" before setting the hook, as our friends from those Commonwealth countries are famous for saying. A fish in skinny water, on the other hand, comes up to smack a dry, and you should give it the business right away. I don't really understand why, but I know this works. Catching fish from deeper water with dries, pause longer on the strike. Fish in skinny water need immediate attention. —**KD**

156. Pride Cometh Before the Fall

Not too long ago, I had surgery on my lower back to correct two compressed vertebrae. One was in such bad shape that it was simply cracked and splitting. I had spacers put in between the repaired bones, and the surgeon drilled six screws into my spine.

It was a long recovery, and it was difficult. But I managed, after several weeks of "light duty," to spend the better part of an Idaho summer walking and wading along my favorite back-country trout streams.

But it wasn't the same. It used to be that I'd just hop off the bank into the creek and start casting. Now, I find myself kind of sitting down on the creek bank and sliding into the water on my butt. It's comical, but it works.

My balance has completely changed. At first, I was worried that I had lost it altogether. Thankfully, I managed to get better at walking over slippery river rocks with practice, but I was reminded that, with age comes certain limitations.

I don't use felt wading boots much, largely because I fish a lot in Yellowstone, and felt is banned for fear that it helps spread aquatic invasive species. But I have taken to using metal studs on my wading boots, and if the boots don't come with studs, I'll drill some short sheet-metal screws into the sole to ensure I have the traction I need.

I haven't graduated to the wading staff, but when the time comes, I will embrace it and get one. I'd rather fish another thirty years than have my fishing career cut short by a spill that I can't recover from. —**CH**

157. **Sheet-Metal Screws**

Speaking of metal studs, sheet-metal screws can turn any pair of rubber- or Vibram-soled wading shoes or boots into more functional footwear for wading. I use quarter-inch sheet-metal screws to avoid too deep a puncture, and I've turned everything from $250 wading boots to $30 sandals into studded footwear using these plentiful and affordable little screws.

I do tend to stay away from felt when I can for fear that it more readily transports invasive organisms like whirling disease and New Zealand mud snails. I also fish quite often in Yellowstone National Park, and felt-soled wading footwear isn't allowed. But, as I get older and a bit less nimble, I've come to realize that I need traction while wading. This is my happy medium. I keep a box of screws and a nut driver in my camper. When I need better footing, this is my solution. —**CH**

158. **Willow Branches Are Great for Balance**

This might sound odd, but I love fishing willow-lined trout streams in the Rockies, and not because of the sweet smell of the native flora or that they provide homes for adult caddis and other aquatic bugs (they do, but that's not the point here).

Instead, I like wading the edges of trout water lined with willows because a handful of willow branches is just as good as a wading staff when you're traversing over slippery rocks. Willows are supple and really strong. On my favorite cutthroat streams here in Idaho, I can maneuver around deep pools, submerged wood, and the like simply by holding on to a few willow branches and using them to help me balance when the footing is suspect.

Most small-stream trout anglers likely know this trick, but for those who haven't tried it, don't hold willows in disdain. Not only do they provide great habitat and streamside shade, they can also help you navigate tricky wading conditions. —**CH**

159. **Wire for Predators**

Pike, bluefish, mackerel, barracuda—they all have teeth, and those teeth will slice right through even the heaviest mono or braid if they come into contact with it. A lot of anglers spurn wire

because it bends after a few uses and can tend to disrupt a retrieve. There was a time when I subscribed to the non-wire philosophy, where I chose to go with heavy monofilament "bite tippets" for pike and even barracuda. I'd had some success without the wire, so I assumed that forty-pound tippet would be just fine.

It wasn't. It was a fool's errand. And, with today's sophisticated wire leaders that are both strong and supple, there's no reason not to use it when you're going after toothy fish. Spend a little extra money and use the wire. You'll save flies (and likely some of the fish that end up swimming off with your fly in its mouth after it's chewed through your leader). —**CH**

160. **Quick-Dry Attire for the Flats**

I've told my buddy Kirk this before: he gave me the best advice I ever got before heading to the tropics to chase bonefish.

"Wear quick-dry underwear," he said. "You'll be a lot more fun to be around."

Hear, hear, brother.

When you're fishing the salt under the tropical sun, two things are guaranteed to happen. First, you're going to sweat. Second, you'll likely end up wet from the waist down, at least once. Equipping your travel bag with undergarments made from quick-dry material will make your fishing more comfortable: You'll dry faster and, for the sake of your fellow angler, you won't smell so bad.

That goes for outerwear, too. If you get wet, you'll get dry faster if you wear the right clothing. —**CH**

161. **ABC. Anything but Cotton**

Speaking of attire, this one's important.

Years ago, a friend of mine and the former owner of Portneuf River Outfitters in Pocatello (now Snake River Fly Shop) told me that when fishing in cold weather and cold water, he abides by one simple rule when it comes to clothing.

"ABC," Roger Thompson told me. "Anything but cotton."

Cotton is absorbent and doesn't dry quickly, meaning once it's wet, it's wet for a while. And in cold weather (I've been known to fish the Henry's Fork in single-degree weather), that can be a real problem. Hypothermia is no joke. For me, when fishing in cold weather, ABC is a rule, not a suggestion. —**CH**

162. **On Fly Line Colors**

Probably the most debated topic with the least consensus in the history of fly fishing. If you bring an orange line anywhere in New Zealand, they'll literally make you take it off your reel and replace it. Orange lines show up better, however, so you can mend them, see your loops, and all that.

I fish tan, moss, brown, and gray lines on fresh water. (Almost always weight-forward, although I fish double tapers on bamboo or fiberglass.) I use blue or tan lines in salt water. I pay less attention to line color in salt than in fresh. The longer your leader, the less fly line colors matter. —**KD**

163. **Sun Protection. It's No Joke**

I'm a fair-skinned, hopelessly white guy with roots in the British Isles and Germany. The sun is not my friend, and years of exposure has me sitting in the dermatologist's chair more than I would like, even though I rarely fish without protection anymore.

Sadly, sun protection—both in the form of SPF creams and lotions and in attire—is often an afterthought for anglers. It shouldn't be. Even trout anglers who fish in more temperate climes should never fish without proper attire. Buffs, face shields, floppy hats, and long sleeves and fishing pants should be regulars in the travel bag, and for when you just hop in the truck for a quick trip to the river. —**CH**

164. **Build Your Own Rod**

Nothing will reinforce your appreciation for today's fly-rod technology than actually building your own fly rod. No, I don't mean that you need to roll your own blank from sheets of fiberglass or graphite, but I do mean it's worthwhile to buy a blank and "assemble" a rod using everything from cork grips to spacing charts to epoxy.

It's a process, and to achieve perfection at it is something to behold. From sanding a grip to attaching double-footed snake guides just so, rod building is an art.

I've built several rods, and I've fished them all. Doing it yourself can save money (only you can determine if the time invested in a rod is worth the money you'll save), and you can truly personalize a fly rod to meet your own preferences. The same blanks that the pros use can be yours for a price, as can the hardware, from the reel-seat insert to your very own custom thread wrapping. In all, you can save significantly when compared to retail, but you have to factor in the experience, too.

Is it easy? I'll say this. It gets easier over time. Is it fun? I enjoy it, but it's not for everyone. It does take time and it does require patience and a steady hand. And, of course, the more you do it, the better you get.

It's definitely an advanced fly-fishing skill, so be sure you're up to the task before you order your parts. —CH

165. **What You Wear Matters**

Several years ago, my friend Corey Fisher—a great angler who lives in Missoula, Montana—and I poked into a little stream in the Gallatin Range of southwest Montana. We were both in Ennis for a work meeting, and we took off late one afternoon and followed a blue line on the map that neither of us had ever fished. I was wearing a red T-shirt—it had been a beautiful summer day, and most of the folks at the meeting were wearing flip-flops, shorts, T-shirts, and the like. Corey was wearing a button-up short-sleeved shirt in God-awful green-and-gold plaid. I actually remember telling him what a hideous color that shirt was.

We parked at the trailhead and hiked maybe a mile through some low-country scabland before we hit the treeline and came upon the little creek that tumbled out of the mountains before it ended up in the Madison. The creek was tiny. Just a trickle. We both knew that if there were fish to be caught, they'd likely be pretty small, too—one of the risks you take when you venture off to explore new water based solely on the lines criss-crossing a map.

I stepped up to the first little pool, and before I even pulled my fly off the rod guide, a small cutthroat dashed for cover. I'd already spooked the hole.

Corey moved up to the next pool, and knelt stealthily. He made a quick cast, and right away a feisty six-inch cutthroat grabbed his small Stimulator fly. I watched him catch a couple more before staking out some new water.

I moved up the creek and gave Corey a half-dozen runs and pools to fish ahead of him. My luck improved, but it wasn't the fact-action fishing I'd expected from backcountry trout that may never see a single fly over the course of a summer. I fished a bit longer and then moved back downstream. Corey was just a couple of pools up from where I left him, and he'd positioned himself among a copse of streamside willows. I think the only reason I saw him was because he moved his arm slightly to make a quick little cast to the head of the pool. His shirt, that eyesore blend of plaid and all, was virtually invisible against the green backdrop.

As we walked out just before dark, and started comparing notes, I realized that Corey had a hell of an afternoon fishing when compared to the half a dozen or so trout I had managed to catch.

"I think it's all in the shirt," I said.

He grinned and put his hand on that horrible button-up shirt.

"Not so hideous after all, huh?"

What you wear matters, especially when you're fishing over wary trout. Even backcountry trout will spy a six-foot, five-inch man wearing a bright red T-shirt and know something's not right.

This is also true on the flats when you're after bonefish or permit. Bright sunny days and a blue sky? I put on a blue or blue-green fishing shirt. Gray skies? Gray or brown shirt.

Match your background and be aware when it changes. You'll be less visible to skittish fish, and more likely to catch them. —**CH**

166. **Ignore Soft-Hackle Flies at Your Own Peril**

Fishing soft-hackles seems to have become something of a lost art. But serious anglers have fly boxes chock full of the soft-hackle versions of popular dry flies that match a river's hatches.

Here in Yellowstone country, I have Blue-winged Olive soft-hackles, Pale Morning Dun soft-hackles, and even larger patterns that are largely attractor patterns.

Craig Mathews, former owner/operator of Blue Ribbon Flies in West Yellowstone, Montana, turned me into a soft-hackle convert in recent years, and my go-to patterns on the fabled Firehole are almost always soft-hackle versions of typical match-the-hatch dries other anglers are using.

I fish soft-hackles on the swing where trout will often see them as emerging insects. One bonus that comes with fishing soft-hackle patterns? Trout will rise to dry flies. They *crush* soft-hackles. —**CH**

167. **Keep a Record of Your Fishing**

Years ago, as I was learning the creeks and streams of my new eastern Idaho home (as of this writing, I've been in Idaho for twenty-one years), I had a little composition notebook that I kept folded inside the dog-eared pages of my DeLorme *Idaho Atlas and Gazetteer*. After fishing, I'd make a note of what happened on that particular day on that particular stream. I recorded everything from the species of fish I caught to the flies I tried. Sometimes I recorded the water temperature, sometimes not, and I made note of the weather, the hatches I noticed, even the wildlife I happened to see while fishing.

While I don't journal as much as I used to, I still reference that old composition notebook often, and I'll journal whenever I fish a new place (which, after more than two decades in the area, isn't very often—I've put in the miles getting to know Idaho). Not only can your journal help you recall what works and what doesn't, it's also a source of great memories. These days, I often laugh at some of the antics my thirty-year-old self was able to pull off that my fifty-year-old self wouldn't even try. —**CH**

168. **Get and Keep a Good Map**

I'm a big fan of the DeLorme Atlas and Gazetteer series. The company makes maps for most states, and while I have shifted a lot of my "research" over to online Google Maps, I still keep

maps for the states I fish the most in my vehicle. They work when data signals don't, and they're easy to mark. When I pair the physical map with the latest in satellite technology, I can really come to understand a watershed that I'm scoping out for a potential fishing trip. —**CH**

169. **One "X" at a Time, If You Please**

When I am building leaders or connecting tippet, I only jump from 3X to 4X, or 4X to 5X, and never jump more than two sizes (like 3X to 6X). A dramatic mismatch of monofilament or fluorocarbon materials is the number one recipe for break-offs, not matter how carefully you tie or test your knots. —**KD**

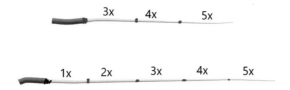

170. **There's a Minimum of a Foot Between Any Knot and Any Dry Fly I Fish**

This doesn't apply so much to nymph rigs, as I think about ten inches is about the perfect distance between the knot (above which I affix my weight, so it won't slide down onto the fly) and the fly itself. But with dry flies, I always have at least a foot, and more like two or three feet, from my leader-to-tippet connector knot (usually a Double Surgeon's) and the fly I fish. This isn't so much because I am afraid a rising trout will see the knot and think it's something spooky, rather, I think the knot can cause micro-drag, which the fish do indeed find spooky or at least unappealing. The more wiggly, supple distance I have from the knot to the fly, the higher my odds of getting bit are, and that's true on semi-flat spring creeks as well as in fast-moving riffles. —**KD**

171. The Strongest Knot Is a Tested Knot

Tom Rosenbauer and the late great *Field&Stream* fishing editor, John Merwin, both told me the same thing, so I will give them equal credit. In short, do not believe anything you read or see in video form or otherwise that tells you that "XYZ knot is 25 percent stronger than ABC knot . . ." While much effort has been expended to determine whether a Blood Knot is a stronger connection than a Double Surgeon's Knot, the honest truth is that anyone who really tries to scientifically measure this runs into so many variables (was the knot properly formed? did you make five twists or four? was the knot lubricated? what diameter of material are you tying with? and so on. . .) that it is impossible to make credible, blanket conclusions. Rosenbauer told me that Orvis once invested in a knot-testing machine, and the range of results was so vast that they mothballed it.

The lesson? Whatever knot you choose, test it before you fish it. Pull on it. Get comfortable with it. Confidence in your knots before you fish is about as important as anything else, because consciously or subconsciously, it affects the way you fish, and especially the way you fight fish when you hook them. —**KD**

172. **Don't Compare Trout to Grizzly Bears**

Another one from Rosenbauer: It's a myth that trout are more likely to eat streamers and big flies in the fall because they are girding up for the winter. "Trout are not grizzly bears," he says. They don't "gird up" for winter. Some species, like brown trout, go into spawning mode in the fall, so they get agitated and will chase, swat, and bite at things that they think might ruin their mojo, which is why you might get more bites on Tim Heng's "Autumn Splendor" pattern in fall (imagine that) than in spring. But if you look at that bug with its wiggly yellow rubber legs, realize that it's not meant to look so much like a cheeseburger as it is meant to look like the carnival clown antagonizing some sucker to take their best shot. —**KD**

173. **A Good Set of Pliers**

For us trout anglers, most of us would think a good set of hemostats is likely all we'll ever need to remove barbless hooks from the mouths of our fish. But for just about every other gamefish—particularly those with teeth or those that swim in salt water—a good set of pliers is a much better option.

And, no, you don't want the work pliers you get at Home Depot. You want heavy-duty stainless-steel pliers that can be

used to reach into a toothy mouth to get deeply hooked flies from the throats of fish. This isn't optional, in my opinion. Having these tools on hand is both good for you, as an angler, and good for the fish you're hoping to release alive. —**CH**

174. **Be a Generalist on the Flats**

A couple years ago, a fishing buddy and I traveled to Xcalak, Mexico, a tiny Yucatán fishing village on the border with Belize. It's one of my favorite tropical do-it-yourself fisheries with access to bonefish and permit flats both on the Caribbean

side and in Chetumal Bay. But it's also an amazing place to cast for jacks off the town dock, tarpon in the marshes, and toothy barracuda that turn up just about anywhere.

We spent a week in Xcalak, and had we just been after bone-fish, we'd have had a blast. We spent one day with a guide on Chetumal Bay, and we quite literally caught bonefish at will. Because I brought several fly rods for different purposes, we also caught snappers, jacks, and 'cudas. I had two shots at permit while wading, and I managed to turn a really nice baby tarpon, too. All because we weren't too keyed in on bones, which were a blast, but, after a spell, a little monotonous (we should all be so lucky, right?).

When you take the time to venture to the tropics to fly fish, remember that bonefish and permit aren't the only gamefish worth chasing (if you've ever hooked a two-foot-long barracuda, you know exactly what I'm talking about). Take the time to pack at least one extra fly rod that can be rigged with a crab pattern for permit, or a streamer for 'cudas, jacks, and tarpon, to go along with your rod rigged with a Gotcha for the bonefish. Chances are you'll encounter potholes, canals, and deeper channels where you'll see fish that might not be on your bucket list (at least not yet), but are more than worthy of a cast or two. —CH

175. Neoprene Socks for Wet Wading

As a younger angler years ago, I was pretty agnostic about my wet-wading footwear. This sort of laissez-faire approach would often result in blisters, scrapes, and bruises on my feet and ankles. But I was young, and the wounds healed quickly. I also thought that these insignificant little injuries were worth the lack of bulk from waders or even wading boots; when a slip-on pair of sandals did the trick, that's what I used.

These days, I'm less inclined to wade wet without a bit more protection. The scrapes and bruises take longer to heal, and the discomfort of fishing through these nagging little injuries mounts up quicker than it used to. Now, I almost always wade wet using wading boots.

But the most important addition to my wet wading has undoubtedly been the neoprene sock or booty. Using these protective socks rather than going with something a little lighter (like wool, for instance) makes all the difference in the world. Not only do they prevent against blisters from wading boots, they also give you a few millimeters of protection from rocks and submerged wood. And, while moving from one fishing spot to another, they give you an extra shield against willow branches, wild roses, and even stinging nettle.

I wish I would have started using neoprene socks years earlier. —**CH**

176. **Respect the Disrespected**

Many years ago, while fishing for brook trout in a remote West Virginia stream, I hooked an odd fish that I couldn't identify. It wasn't a trout, and it wasn't a bass. Back home in the West, I might have called it a creek chub, but it wasn't quite that, either. My friend Bryan Moore, who had delivered me to his little slice

of "almost heaven," quickly identified the 10-inch critter wriggling at the end of my tippet.

"It's a fall fish," he said. Fall fish are native to Appalachia, from the mid-Atlantic region north through New England and into Canada. They fight well and they'll hit a fly. And, as it turns out, they are indeed a variety of chub and come from the *cyprinadae* family (just like carp). Bryan was quick to point out that a lot of anglers throw fall fish back . . . as in "back over their shoulders into the woods."

The poor fall fish, it seems, shares the same branding challenge of our mountain whitefish here in the Rockies. Whitefish are salmonids, just like trout. Their closest relative is the Arctic grayling (and no, they don't look nearly as lovely as the lacy grayling). But they are native. And, not unlike the fall fish, they are an indicator species that require good habitat to survive and thrive.

As a bonus to us fly fishers, whitefish are game fighters and will often hit a fly when trout might be close-lipped, particularly in winter. They can be found on some of the West's best trophy trout streams, from the Roaring Fork to the Madison and, as a native and telltale indicator of water quality, they deserve a bit of respect.

Throw them back, indeed. Into the water from which they came. —**CH**

177. **Give Mitten Clamps a Try, Even Without Mittens**

I love a good pair of hemostats, but they're often not up to the job. They're also confining if you use them as intended, with your fingers in the closed-circle grips. I've taken to almost exclusively using more sturdy "mitten clamps," even when I'm not wearing mittens.

The premise is the same: You're able to reach into fish mouths, clamp down on a hook, and safely remove a fly, just as you would with your traditional hemostats. But they simply function better, mostly because they have a spring-loaded grip that, when you release the clamp, pushes the jaws apart for you. Hemostats don't do that.

Also, mitten clamps don't come with finger grips—you squeeze them as you would a pair of pliers. Second, they're stronger and sturdier. I've even used them in the salt when I forgot my good saltwater pliers. They weren't ideal, but they worked just fine.

Finally, just like hemos, you can lock and unlock them from your vest, chest pack, or sling pack with relative ease without having to slide your fingers into the circle grips. As a bonus, my mitten clamps also have a heavy-duty set of cutters that are stronger than regular nippers and can handle small-gauge wire.

What's not to like about them? Next time you get your fingers snared in a set of hemos like a Chinese finger trap when you're trying to remove a hook, remember . . . I told you so. —**CH**

178. **Don't Ignore the Town Dock**

A couple years back, on what turned out to be one of the best DIY fishing trips of my life, my fishing buddy and I spent the better part of each evening in the little Yucatán village of Xcalak casting from the big concrete town dock. After each day spent poking around the beaches and the flats of Chetumal Bay, we'd pour a rum punch cocktail and walk down the dock armed

with a 7-weight and pockets full of Clousers. Often, this was the best fishing of the day, and it was always fun to see what might hit a fly at any given time.

The "town dock" is germane to many little fishing villages, but there are docks everywhere, and not just in salt water. As a kid, some of my best fishing for white bass, bream, and crappie was around the boat docks and slips of Lake Tyler in east Texas. I spent a memorable night with a guide on Tampa Bay casting to snook, redfish, and trout that congregated under the lights along the docks belonging to multimillion-dollar mansions. Here in Idaho, the best early season bass fishing in some of our lower-elevation lakes is usually found along floating docks.

It makes sense. Fish need structure, both for food and security. If you're not making a few casts along that structure, you're missing an opportunity. —**CH**

179. **The Beach Can Be a Blast**

I have really come to enjoy saltwater fly fishing, and while it's fashionable to try and go to far-flung flats in distant lands (and that's a lot of fun, to be sure), I've found that some of the best fishing I've enjoyed is often right off the beach in some popular places right here in the US.

One October, a fishing friend and I spent a memorable afternoon casting to and catching speckled trout right off the beach on Sanibel Island in Florida. On the Emerald Coast near Destin, Florida, I had a heyday casting Schminnows to leaping ladyfish, lizardfish, and small jacks. In Texas' Laguna Madre, I enjoyed a stellar January day catching redfish and speckled trout within view of the bayside mansions and condos where folks were busy sunbathing and enjoying cocktails by the pool.

Often, walking a beach and looking for bait and diving birds can put you in touch with some great inshore fishing, without the need to spring for a guide or a boat. Beaches, particularly where the break is soft, can be amazing places to cast flies, and they offer great variety for the shore-bound angler. —CH

180. "Go Deep in the Name of Trout Research"

I've spent many hours in scuba gear, hanging on to rocks in rivers, just watching trout eat. Snorkeling is cool and informative, but you're always bobbing up and down, just to breathe, and that's not as steady a baseline as being able to spend an hour on the bottom of a run. I won't go into the details of that article, which appeared in *Field & Stream*, but these were the six main takeaways. 1) I was amazed that I could get so close to fish (within arm's reach) and watch them in a normal routine. Why? Because trout aren't used to a six-foot-long, neoprene-clad, bubble-blowing blob hanging out with them! They don't know how to process that situation. 2) What does spook them most of all (and it is not close) are shadows and motions overhead. Think about that the next time you are false casting over a fish, and always consider the sun's position. 3) A great nymph angler misses 50 percent of strikes. 4) Most trout won't move more than a vertical foot to eat a nymph fly. Emergers and dries are different stories, but nymph fishing is all about weight and depth. 5) Yarn indicators look more "natural" from below and they make less noise when they land than bobber indicators. And . . . 6) Even after a fish is disturbed and gets off its routine (as in, they've just had a kayak go over them), it takes seconds, maybe minutes for them to settle back into a routine. So don't sweat the tubers. —**KD**

181. The Underappreciated Ladyfish

Along the coast of Florida, from the Emerald Coast all the way to Florida Bay, a great fly-rod fish hammers flies and entertains anglers almost every day of the year. Yet you almost never hear about the ladyfish.

The first ladyfish I caught was in a remote canal that connected a series of salt flats in the Bahamas. I was on my first-ever bonefish trip, and the weather we managed to dial up in March was absolutely brutal: sideways rain, thirty-knot wind, and almost a week solid of cloud cover. I really struggled with the bonefish, but I had blast catching baby tarpon, mangrove snappers, barracuda, and ladyfish from the canals that boats used to get from one flats complex to the other.

The biggest ladyfish I ever caught was along the East Cape of the Baja; it might have been twenty inches long. But it pulled

hard, cartwheeled out of the water a few times, and really put on a show. One fall, off the beach at Captiva Island in southwest Florida, I spent a full day playing with ladyfish that were absolutely acrobatic.

Along the south Texas coast, near the border with Mexico, ladyfish are called skipjacks, and just like anywhere else, they are great fun on a fly rod. They're generally reachable along beaches and bays and, for the most part, anglers don't need a boat to get to them.

Ladyfish are in the *Elopidae* family (just like tarpon and bonefish). If you're fishing waters where ladyfish are present, you'd be wise to add a hefty length of thirty-pound bite tippet. Their teeth are small, but they're very sharp. —**CH**

182. What I Really Think About the Bobber/Strike Indicator

I think it's an incredibly effective way to hook fish. I think that's great in the context that someone wants to feel the tug of a fish. I think it's a great way for guides to get people pulling on fish, and hopefully enjoy that so much that they get interested in fly fishing. When nothing else is going on, and I really want to hook fish, or more often I want someone I'm fishing with to pull on a fish, I put on a nymph rig. And I do think there's a real benefit to understanding and mastering nymphing, especially now, when so many other anglers nymph fish by default.

That's pretty much where the compliments end. What I really think is that nymph fishing is riding a bike with training wheels. If you go anywhere else in the world to fish for big trout, almost all the guides and locals recoil at the thought of

fishing a double-nymph rig with a weight down low and an indicator up top. So long as they don't "have to" do that, they won't do it. —**KD**

183. **Glass Is Back**

As a kid, my fishing rods were all fiberglass—noodly, flexible, and sensitive glass. As technology has evolved, particularly over the last thirty years or so, glass rods have, sadly, become somewhat passé. That's too bad. Fiberglass rods still have a place in fly fishing, and devotees of the material scorn today's faster graphite rods in favor of slower, "old-school" fly rods crafted from quality fiberglass.

Glass rods have evolved. No longer are fiberglass fishing rods heavy and bulky: Some high-end glass rods are downright weightless, and, particularly for small-game rods (think fly rods in 1- to 4-weight class), they can be better implements for precision angling situations. That's not to say they're inappropriate for big-game situations (bass, saltwater fish, etc.), but glass rods are slower and require anglers to adjust their cast accordingly.

In small-stream situations, I really enjoy fishing a wispy glass rod more than I do even the highest-end graphite. There may be nothing better for delicate presentations and up-close angling situations than a really fine stretch of glass.

If you haven't tried glass lately, and maybe you're a little "glass-curious" as the material continues to make a comeback, give it a whirl. I think you'll find that, after you slow your cast and get a feel for more flexible material, you'll realize that you're not really sacrificing much (if at all) in terms of accuracy. You might not be able to throw eighty feet of line into a twenty-knot wind at a cruising bonefish, but you can certainly put a dry fly on target in just about any trout stream. —CH

184. Twelve of the Best Fly-Fishing Destinations in the World, Summarized in One Paragraph

1. New Zealand. Epic, stunningly beautiful, and the best big-trout sight fishing in the world, especially on the South Island. It's ten times harder than most American

anglers anticipate it being, so if you don't have a single-digit fishing "handicap" you won't catch many fish (but you'll still love the country). There's nothing there that wants to bite you, eat you, kill you, poison you, and so forth, so it's literally like fishing in a fairy tale.

2. Tasmania, Australia. Overlooked, underappreciated, and wide open, but the trout in shallow lakes cruise, wake, and tail like seven-pound bonefish, and they'll eat dry flies. Bring long hemostats to pull your tongue back up your throat after your first encounter with a tiger snake (should *not* be a deal-breaker, but you should be aware). Probably the strongest angling tradition and community anywhere in the world.

3. Kamchatka, Russia. Not at all like the "Russian version of Alaska," which is what I had envisioned. You will be about as far from the comforts of home—and at the same time immersed in virgin wilderness—as you can be anywhere on the planet that isn't covered by an ice cap. Do your homework, only go with the most dialed, reputable outfitters, and even then, have contingency plans. Hands down the best mouse fishing in the world, perhaps the last place that demonstrates how predatory unpressured trout really can be.

4. The American Rockies. The envy of all the other angling communities around the world, literally, because of the sheer vastness of opportunities—miles of rivers, and millions of land acres, available to the public, for free. You can catch just as big trout in the West as you can in Chile or Argentina, and so on—maybe not as many, and you might have to get off the beaten path—but they're

here. The diversity of native species is incredible, and worthy of trying to experience as much as possible in an angling lifetime.

5. Alaska. Every American angler should try to experience Alaska at least once in their lives, if only to see just how wild and beautiful it is. Fishing-wise, it's a very large, geographically diverse state, and impossible to lock in on one spot as "quintessential" Alaska. I've been fortunate to visit many times and if I were told I could only go back once more, I would either go to Kodiak Island or the Bristol Bay region. All salmon seasons are great, but my favorite time is when the silvers run and the rainbow trout are fattest.

6. Iceland. Unquestionably the most visually captivating natural landscape of anywhere I have ever fished. The native brown trout fishing can be as good or better than the legendary Atlantic salmon beats, and brown trout fishing can cost considerably less. But everything is expensive in Iceland, particularly the food and drink. Regardless of what anyone tells you, that traditional fermented shark stuff is absolutely gross, no matter how much of the local liqueur you drink.

7. Amazon rain forest. Fishing the Amazon today is what hunting in Africa during the golden age of the Big Five safari was over a century ago. It might be the last, wildest place for exploratory fishing, and we're just learning what the fish are like, what they eat, and how to catch them. This might also be the place in the world that could benefit most by using fishing as an economic driver—to protect the rain forest and benefit

indigenous people. If you go there, you will still hear the jungle after you come home . . . for weeks when you dream at night . . . it's weird and wonderful.

8. Argentina (Tierra del Fuego). Sea-run browns thrive here like nowhere else on earth. One guide I met at a certain lodge got sent home to America after his first day on the job because he parked downwind, and the steady 60-mph breeze blew the door off his truck when he opened it. Food and wines are awesome, fishing is grueling but rewarding, and I'd rate this as one of those places you'd aspire to check off once or twice, but it takes serious game, grit, and money to make TDF a habit.

9. Argentina (Patagonia). If you imagine what Montana might have been, fishing-wise, at the time Norman Maclean grew up and fished there, minus the telephone lines, billboards, and paved highways . . . that's what Patagonia seems to me. You're probably not going to catch a trout much larger than something you could catch in Montana or Michigan, but you can experience solitude. And it's pretty darn nice to experience summer in January.

10. Ireland. Greatest place I have ever fished—greatest people, culture, music, and overall experience—in the context that I didn't actually care about catching fish. It can be epic on private water, with stocked brown trout, and such, but the wild fishery is still challenged, though rebounding. None of that matters. it's an absolutely soul-captivating place, and a notable omission for any angler with even distant Irish familial roots. Do fish the lakes.

11. Bahamas. The hands-down place to fish if you want to catch bonefish. It's so close to the American mainland, and the people and guide culture are fantastic. Bonefish tend to be bigger here, and they are not "gimmes." There is always wind. But it is silly to travel halfway around the world to chase bones or any other saltwater species until you have spent at least ten quality trips in the Bahamas.

12. Belize. Pretty much ditto everything I just said on the Bahamas, though the fish tend to be just a tad smaller, yet the cast-for-cast opportunities tend to be a tad higher. And depending where you go, Belize also offers permit and tarpon. If you are a glutton for punishment and want to chase permit, there is no other place I'd choose above Belize. But I'd be really strategic about the seasons. I'd also spend at least three days inland before hitting the flats. The jungle and Mayan ruins are incredible. —**KD**

185. $90 or $900 . . . You Choose

The fly-rod companies don't want me saying this, but the fly-line companies do. And since many of them are in those same businesses at the same time, I figure it's worth putting out there. A new, clean $80 fly line will do more to make your cast dance than a new $900 fly rod ever will. I'm certainly a sucker for the sales pitches, and I want the newest rods with the best tapers, and space-age resins and all that, but if I put a new line on my twenty-year-old rod that I've been fishing (and am comfortable with),

I'll cast that better than I will a new rod fresh out of the tube. Been there, done that many times. —**KD**

186. **Electrical Tape on the Grip**

My friend Al Quattrocchi is one of the pioneers on the California surf-fly-fishing scene (a real corbina guru), and he's always tinkering around with running lines and shooting lines. He's the same as a lot of steelheaders who throw two-handers, and want all the weight in the line, up in the head, and then back down to a stiffer, lower diameter material like Amnesia, or even just heavy Maxima or monofilament. If you do that, you can chew up your fingers, so I tend to wear finger guards or just tape up. But you can also lose braking control on the line as you try to pinch it with your taped fingers against the grip of your rod. Al's solution is simply a few wraps of electrical tape at the tip of the grip. It doesn't stick like duct tape, and can be removed and replaced without marking up your rod. And it serves as a really effective "brake pad" when you are fighting larger fish. —**KD**

187. **I Cheer for the Fish**

At the end of the day, I must tell you, I ultimately cheer for fish. Even when I'm trying to catch them. Years ago, I used to get all mad if a big trout wrapped me around a stump, or a tarpon spit out the fly. Now I just smile, because I know I still have a lot to learn. And I truly respect the fish.

It's okay to lose sometimes, because that's how you learn. That might be the biggest change in my fishing attitude over the

past ten years. The more you fish, and the more you experience, the more you cheer for the fish. —**KD**

188. Get Comfortable in All Kinds of Boats

Some years back, while fishing the New River near Roanoke, Virginia, a good buddy and I ended up fishing from a canoe together. Both of us are western anglers, and we're definitely more comfortable in a driftboat than in something that's tippier. And, predictably, about halfway through the trip, we went over a small rapid and ended up in the water. It was then and there that I decided, if I was to fish for varied species and have success, I first had to become somewhat adept at fishing from boats that weren't reliably stable rafts or dories. I've put in time in both kayaks and canoes and, truth be told, I'd almost rather fish from a kayak than from any other kind of boat. It can be easy to maneuver and, with some practice, very agile—and with just a little practice, super stable. I still struggle a bit with canoes, but I've gotten better. Once, several years ago, I had a great day fishing the Delta Clearwater River from a canoe for grayling in Alaska. Solo, I turned the canoe so I was sitting essentially in the bow and facing the stern. I moved a bit forward from the bow seat and knelt on my knees, putting more of my weight toward the middle of the boat. Then, because I'm right-handed, I moved slightly to the right in the canoe so my stroke could be almost perfectly vertical. It took some getting used to, but I no longer approach a day in a canoe with apprehension. I wish I'd had this knowledge that summer day in Virginia all those years ago. —CH

189. **Keep Fish in the Water**

There are all sorts of new rules about how to handle fish when we bring them in. But, of late, I've decided to become a bit more evangelical on this topic, and I can thank my great friend Sam Davidson, an amazing fly angler from California, for the lesson and for frequent reminders.

I remembered back a few years when Sam and I met on the Trinity River in northern California and spent a long weekend chasing "half-pounders." Half-pounders are early-run steelhead that, rather than spend two or three years in the ocean, might make a spawning run after a single season in the salt.

THE LITTLE BLACK BOOK OF FLY FISHING

They're chrome-bright, absolutely stunning, and they fight like hell. And we had a pretty good weekend playing with them. I noticed, however, that Sam never took the trout out of the water to remove the hook. Instead, with steady hands befitting a surgeon, he carefully used a set of hemostats to grip the base of the fly in the fish's mouth and gingerly worked it free, usually while cradling the fish with his other hand.

I asked him about his release technique.

"It's simple," he said to me recently. "Fish shouldn't ever come out of the water."

Simple, yes, but in today's grip-and-grin world where entire Instagram accounts depend on anglers boastfully holding fish out of the water, it seems kind of . . . absolute. And I'm not the best role model—the marketing material for a lodge on Reindeer Lake in Saskatchewan features a photo of me holding a giant pike well out of the water and sporting that perfect "social media" grin.

But times change. Trout, in particular, face myriad threats. Everything from climate change to compromised habitat is conspiring to give many trout populations a troubling long-term diagnosis. Some biologists predict that we'll lose about 50 percent of all trout habitat in the United States by the middle of this century. That's less than thirty years away.

So let's give them one less threat. Keep them in the water whenever you can. —CH

190. Leave the Rocks Alone

In recent years, I've seen more and more rock cairns constructed on stream banks when I fish on public lands. It's likely that's because fly fishing is a growing pastime, and there are more people out and about casting flies to trout. Harmless? Largely, yes (but a solid argument could be made that constructing the rock towers does, indeed, disturb habitat and possibly even kill some aquatic insects).

But the cairns, at least to me, deliver a more pointed message. Something like, "I was here before you were, and I built this little monument to mark my conquest."

I take great pleasure knocking down cairns and redistributing streamside rocks. To me, building a cairn is the less-permanent equivalent of defacing a cliff face with a can of spray paint. The fewer people who know you were there, the better. Leave the rocks alone. —**CH**

191. **The Dreaded Hashtag**

We live in a world where a single photograph can forever alter a landscape. In today's social-media environment, an "@" and a "#" can spell doom for a single fishery. Posting a photo of a small creek in, say, West Virginia, describing its great brook trout fishing and then tagging the photo with the name of the creek could, indeed, invite disaster. A few more anglers visiting and fishing a little-known gem could change the destination altogether.

Oddly, I used to be a "share and share alike" kind of guy. Hell, I've written three fly-fishing guidebooks. But not anymore. After witnessing a small stream not too far from home get pounded over the course of a few summers thanks to its population of big cutthroats and the social media mavens who had to share its secrets, I don't tag locations anymore when I post a fishing photo. We're at the precipice of a significant growth spurt in fly fishing, and while I'd love for everyone new to the craft to enjoy success and come to love the pastime, I also think that I'll be keeping more of my favorite fishing destinations to myself. I just don't trust social media . . . or the people who use it irresponsibly. —**CH**

192. **Take the Temperature**

When you step into a trout stream, do yourself and the trout a favor and take the water's temperature. Ideally, for trout, temperatures would be somewhere in the low to mid-fifties—that's when trout are the most active and when they're most likely to be feeding. As summer progresses, keep that thermometer handy, and if you start to see water temperatures climbing above 60°F, consider taking a break . . . and giving a break to the trout. Hooking, playing, and releasing a trout is one of the most stressful things that fish will ever endure. Higher water temperatures add to that stress.

For most trout—there are some evolutionary exceptions to the rule—water temperatures over 70°F will prove fatal in time. It's important that we, as anglers, literally keep our fingers on the pulse of our trout rivers. When we notice that they're warming up into that danger zone, we should do something else. Skip rocks or wander back to camp and enjoy a cold beer. Just don't tempt trout when the fight might be the last thing they ever do. —**CH**

193. **Consider a Camp Trailer**

Several years back, I bought a small camper and drove from my home in Idaho Falls all the way to the Arctic Ocean and then back, fishing at every possible opportunity. It was my trip of a lifetime, and I thoroughly enjoyed the ten-week adventure. I used the camper religiously when I got home from that journey. It was compact and made for "boondocking," or camping in areas where there is no water, sewer, or electricity. It was easily the best purchase I ever made, and it helped me stay in the hills for days at a time and in relative comfort.

RVs aren't for everyone. But, as I grew older, the thought of a daily shower and the ability to poop indoors were just too appealing to ignore. The average camp trailer is an engineering marvel—the ability to cram so much capability into such a small space is a testament to modern vehicle construction. Of course, one can overdo it, and go big and bulky and end up with too much of a good thing. If you're RV-curious and you like to fish, particularly on public lands, consider renting one for a weekend just to see if you like it. If you're at all like me, it will become your mobile fishing station. My little camper served as a lockable fly-fishing outfitter lodge on wheels, and I've towed it across the continent in search of fish. I may not always have a boat . . . but I'll always have a camper. For an angler, that's saying something. —CH

194. Use the Fly Shop Appropriately

Local fly shops have one thing going for them that just can't be found if you choose to buy flies and equipment online: local knowledge.

A good fly shop proprietor does everything she or he can do to make a fly-fishing outing a success for customers, up to including sharing the fly patterns that are working on particular waters and where to go to ensure success. But don't just pop in, ask questions, and leave. That's a major party foul.

Instead, make a purchase—even a small one. Be friendly and engaging and ask good questions, like, "What size BWO are they hitting on the South Fork?" or "Where would you go with a new fly angler so they might have some success?" Be specific and courteous, and don't monopolize a proprietor's time.

I can't think of a time when I've been disappointed by a visit to the local shop, even if it was just for a spool of tippet or some tying materials. I know my local proprietor, but when I travel, I still make a point to at least ask a few questions about my intended destination, and the best place to do that is at the fly shop. Now and then, I'll pick up some intel that saves my trip. For instance, every time I go to Yellowstone National Park to fish, I pop into Blue Ribbon Flies and, if I'm lucky, Craig Mathews or John Juracek will be there, and I can pick their brains about my plans for the day. Some years back, Craig shifted my focus from fishing the Firehole because a warm spell had caused the river to warm up too quickly, and most of the fish were retreating into cooler tributaries. So I chose to fish a small backcountry lake, instead. For the price of a half-dozen flies, my day got a lot better.

Fly-shop owners and employees are the ambassadors for fly fishing and for the local waters they represent. Thinking of a fly shop as just a place to buy flies is a mistake. A good fly shop will be the hub of any successful fishing trip. —**CH**

195. **Take Care of Your Fishing Buddy**

I've always had "fishing dogs." Let's face it. Life is better with a good dog in it. And, frankly, where I like to fish, a good dog can prove to be really helpful. Years ago, while hiking out of a steep canyon on the fringes of Yellowstone National Park, my old fishing buddy, Spooner, got between me and a sow grizzly who bluff-charged me as I eclipsed the lip of the canyon and surprised her and her two cubs. The dog barked and growled and stood his ground. The bear, realizing I meant no harm to her or her brood, stopped her charge about ten yards short, rounded up her cubs, and trotted off into the timber.

The experience was harrowing, and I can only imagine how it might have ended if Spooner hadn't been with me. Honestly, I was so winded from the climb out of the canyon that I may not have even seen the bear until it was too late.

If you have a good fishing dog, do your part and take care of him or her. Some years back, while fishing for carp in southern Idaho's Snake River, I noticed an abundance of ticks had found their way onto Phoebe, my old fishing mutt of questionable origin. I did my best to brush the critters off her, and when we got home, I shampooed her with a flea-and-tick concoction. Nevertheless, a couple of days later, I still had to pick several swollen ticks off my dog. I felt horrible.

Now, every spring, Phoebe sports a brand-new tick collar, and before we head off into the field, she gets a spray of tick repellant. She's getting older right along with me, so she also gets some treats that have glucosamine and chondroitin in them to help keep her joints loose and lubricated. And, if it's just the two of us in the camper, I boost her up and let her sleep on the bed. She eats high-quality food when we go camping and fishing, and she always has a bowl full of fresh water. Always.

Phoebe lives to go fishing, and she'll walk anywhere I walk in search of fish. She's my constant fishing companion—if I try and give her a break by leaving her at camp with my girlfriend, it's only a matter of time before she makes a break for it and finds me by the creek. I do my best to take care of her, so she'll be able to fish with me for a while yet, and sometimes that means not taking her along, no matter how much it breaks my heart.

I know she won't last forever—dogs come and go so quickly over the course of our lives—but I do want to make her short time with me count. So I do my best to make sure she's comfortable and healthy. It's the least I can do. —CH

196. Listen to (and Watch) the Gear Folks

Fly fishers tend to pigeonhole themselves and often fail to participate in larger conversations about fishing in general. Granted, there are some aspects of baitcasting and spinfishing that just aren't germane to fly anglers. But, on the whole, good information presented by bait and spin anglers can be beneficial to those of us who pursue fish with the long rod.

Examples? When you travel to a new and unfamiliar destination, it pays to join local and regional online message boards. Often, hot fishing locales and water conditions can be gleaned from these sites, and that data is just as useful to fly fishers as it is to conventional anglers. The same is true for bait and lures. If the shrimp bite is going gangbusters just off the beach, you have a pretty good idea what fly to use when you visit, right?

If you fish with gear anglers, pay attention when they start catching fish. How deep is their lure or bait? What color is that plug that caught that bass? How fast was that lure retrieved? You're likely not going to be able to match a really good spin angler fish for fish, but if you pay attention to the things that make them successful, you can learn a lot about how the fish are behaving, where you might find them, and what you should have on your tippet. —**CH**

197. Makos Will Teach You How to Fight Fish

Fly fishing is not an extreme sport. Bull riding is an extreme sport. Fly fishing is not . . . with one exception. Fly fishing for mako sharks is the last stop on the sanity express. My friend Conway Bowman introduced me to the madness many years ago, and I've never been able to kick that habit since. If you want to learn how to fight really big fish with a fly rod, using the line and a low rod angle, bowing during jumps and all that, makos are the best teachers in the world, because they can swim sixty miles per hour and jump more than twice their body length above the surface. Imagine tying a line to a two-hundred-pound NFL wide receiver . . . only the shark swims three times faster than the NFL player runs, covering the length of a football field in a few seconds, and when it reaches the end zone, it jumps over the crossbar a few times. —**KD**

198. Here's Mud on Your Fly

Capt. Markk Cartwright, a guide out of Dead Man's Cay on Long Island in the Bahamas, is convinced that bonefish have the most acute senses of any fish on the flats (I might argue that permit are even more tuned in to what's happening around them),

and that, in order to consistently fool them, anglers need to consider all factors involved in the process. Yes, you need that solid cast, and the presentation must be just so . . . but Cartwright believes it's the little things that make the difference for picky bones, and it starts by eliminating the elements that work against anglers.

While I've always tried to control the things I can control—the lens tint on my sunglasses, the color of the shirt I wear to reduce the impact of my silhouette, tippet size, the size of the fly and its weight, etc.—Cartwright takes it a step further. Before he even stretches his fly line in preparation for a day of walking and wading the flats, he takes his fly and buries it in the mud or the sand of the flats. This, he says, removes any odors that might make the fly less appealing to a cruising bone. Think about it . . . threads, tinsels, feathers, and, of course, the chemicals in head cement or UV resin all have scents attached to them. Burying the fly for a second or two in the bottom of the flats might reduce or remove some of those unnatural scents.

When bonefish are finicky and spooky, which they very often are, sometimes it's the little things that make the difference between a refusal and a hookup. Remove one of the little things. Bury your fly. —**CH**

199. How to Know If a Fish Is in Trouble

There are tells that will show you when almost any fish, from the cold river to the ocean, is significantly stressed to the point that it may not survive. These fish need extra TLC to be revived. But it's important not to get in the habit of trying to revive every fish that doesn't need it—in those cases, you're overhandling a fish that would be fine if you just let it swim away. If you go to www.keepfishwet.org you'll find a wealth of science-based information on best catch-and-release practices.

So, how do you know when a trout you catch needs extra help, like pointing it upstream in the current to get water (and oxygen) flowing through its gills? Dr. Andy Danylchuk showed me a number of things, but three signs really stuck out most. Remember:

1. If a fish can swim away on its own, let it. If you're gently gripping it by the tail, and it wiggles as if to swim away, that's good. If it just sits there, it might need help.

2. If you tilt a fish back and forth, its eye should roll, almost tracking you. If its eyes demonstrate a blank, fixed stare without movement, that's a problem.

3. If the trout cannot right itself if you roll it on its side, within three seconds, that's another problem.

If those things happen, you might go into revival mode, keeping the fish in the water in your rubberized net, facing into the gentle current, still handling with wet hands as little and as softly as possible. And when they do want to swim away, let them do it. —**KD**

200. **Travel Simple**

I've learned a number of lessons during all my fishing travels (some the hard way). Here are what I consider the most important five: First, mosquitoes are the most dangerous animals in the world, more so than any bear, shark, or snake. So, pay attention to vaccination recommendations and bring bug dope (but never pack that anywhere near your fly line). Second, the highest risk of you getting sick or injured is caused by your paying too much attention to fishing and not enough on staying in the game. Always keep hydrated and wear sunscreen/appropriate clothing. Third, I always bring at least one extra fly line and at least a dozen patterns of every fly pattern I fish (because there is nothing worse than running out of the hot bug). Four, I always bring three tints of polarized glasses—one for bright, one for overcast/low-light and an "in-between" pair in case you lose either of the others. And five, I love the BOA closure system on boots, but never travel with them. Laces are so much easier to fix or replace. Always travel with spare laces. —**KD**

201. **Listen to the Fish, Not Just Us**

Probably the best piece of advice we can give you is to trust yourself or, more important, to trust the water, the fish, and what they tell you. You can read any book, any magazine article—watch any video, read any blog, or any of that stuff—and it all inevitably changes at the exact moment when you step out into the water and make ready for that first cast. All we have aspired to do with this book is to put you in a place where you can improvise and make a plan for yourself. We totally stand by everything we said here, and all we want to do is help. But the overriding lesson is that it is all such a gray area. There are no black-and-white rules to follow every single time, in every single situation. Use all the colors . . . all the victories . . . all the failures . . . and meld those into an approach, or several approaches. But most important, use your eyes and watch what is happening, and follow the fish. You will never, ever, find a better guide than the fish themselves, and the number one prerequisite for being a great angler is having enough information and on-the-water experiences to fuel your own mind, and at the same time being smart enough to let the fish and what you see in front of you channel that knowledge. —**KD**